WOMEN WAR ARTISTS

Kathleen Palmer

Tate Publishing

Imperial War Museum

Special thanks to the artists and their families who have been so generous in supplying images and biographical information, granting copyright permissions and making insightful comments.

Thanks to Angela Weight and Brian Foss, and also to Tate's peer reviewer for detailed and helpful comments and advice. Thanks to my Dad, Michael Stokes, for his comments as a non-specialist reader.

Thanks to many colleagues at the Imperial War Museum for all their help and support, including: all of the Art team – in particular Sara Bevan who researched and wrote artist biographies and compiled tables as well as being a valuable sounding board; Amanda Mason, for additional biographical research; Suzanne Bardgett, Head of Research, for encouragement and feedback; Rebecca Hunter for her design; Madeleine James and Peter Taylor in the Publishing team.

Particular thanks to my husband Jeremy and my young sons James and Alex for their support and forbearance.

First published 2011 by order of the Tate Trustees
by Tate Publishing, a division of Tate Enterprises Ltd,
Millbank, London SW1P 4RG
www.tate.org.uk/publishing

on the occasion of the exhibition
Women War Artists

Imperial War Museum London 9 April 2011 – 8 January 2012
www.iwm.org.uk

A catalogue record for this book is available from the British Library

ISBN 978 1 85437 989 4

Printed by Graphicom SrL

Contents

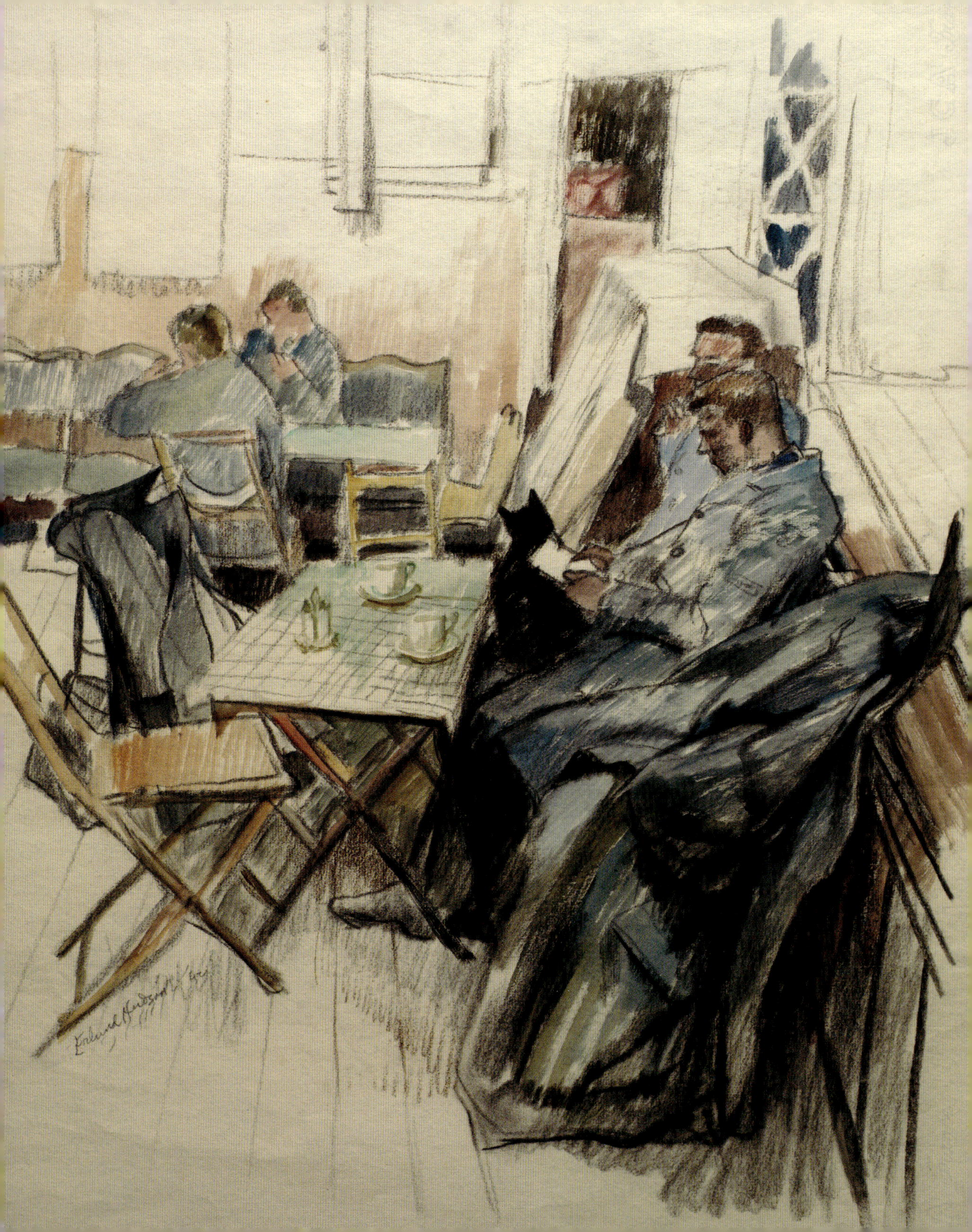

Introduction

When considering 'war art', the paintings that spring most readily to mind are those of the great artists of the First World War, such as Paul Nash, C.R.W. Nevinson, William Orpen and John Singer Sargent. In the Second World War one might think of Henry Moore, Stanley Spencer or Eric Ravilious. Few people could name a woman artist from either conflict.

The stereotypical view of a war artist is someone working at the front line, capturing the brutality of combat or the landscape of battle, sketchbook in hand. The reality was and is rather different, but it is this simplistic view of war artists that has tended to eclipse the role of women artists in portraying war and conflict. The emphasis on artists at the front line means that contemporary art addressing conflict is often not considered as war art at all, although its creators include many well-known women artists.

War art encompasses far more than battle scenes, or life at the front line – it is about artists' creative responses to all aspects of war as seen and experienced by ordinary people, civilians as well as servicemen and women. One of the great strengths of British official war art of the two World Wars is its broad scope, and its encyclopaedic approach to recording total war. A whole range of talented artists – some well established, others early in their careers – were offered the opportunity to respond to a wide spectrum of subjects both in the war zone and at home. The fundamental shift in the technology and practice of war since 1945 has also led to changes in the way official commissioning operates, and how artists have adapted to new restrictions and dangers. Nevertheless, artists continue to find war a subject worthy of exploration. Increasingly they take a more analytical, conceptual approach, investigating the morality of war, challenging social attitudes or pursuing themes such as history and memory.

Women have been commissioned through official war art schemes since the First World War. However, their experiences and treatment have until recently differed significantly from that of their male counterparts, with fewer opportunities to venture beyond the domestic, social and industrial subjects on the home front that were deemed suitable for them. But despite their absence from foreign fields, their contribution has greatly enriched our knowledge and understanding of life in wartime. In this context the achievements of artists such as Anna Airy, Evelyn Dunbar, Dame Laura Knight and Linda Kitson deserve to be more widely acknowledged.

Eleanor (Erlund) Hudson

Forces Canteen 1942

The first official war artists' scheme was set up by the British government in 1916. Started mainly for propaganda purposes, it soon developed higher and more artistic aims – to both record and memorialise Britain's war effort. Only four women were commissioned through this scheme, compared with forty-seven men.[1] Of these four, three artists had their work rejected, and one did not take up the commission. Although artists were paid according to a scale of fixed rates, terms for women artists were stricter, with tight deadlines and penalty clauses for late delivery. This reflects social attitudes to women at this time, but is still surprising given the recognition and standing enjoyed by the artists involved.

It was left to the Imperial War Museum (IWM)'s Women's Work Sub-committee (WWS) to ensure official representation for women artists. Established immediately after the war to collect material on women's war work, this female-run committee commissioned nine painters, a photographer and a number of sculptors, all of them women, as well as a number of male artists. However in the government scheme and IWM commissions together, women made up only five per cent of the official artists in the First World War. In the 1919 exhibition *The Imperial War Museum – The Nation's War Paintings and Other Records* at the Royal Academy, of the 925 works on show just fifteen paintings and a small number of sculptural models were by women. There was almost no comment in the press on their work.

In the Second World War a single, comprehensive government scheme was established under the auspices of the Ministry of Information. The War Artists Advisory Committee (WAAC) was responsible for the commission or purchase of over 5,000 works of art; some were distributed to museums, galleries and other institutions around Britain and the Empire, but the majority – over 3,000 – came to the IWM. More than 400 artists were involved, of whom fifty-two were women – just under thirteen per cent.[2] Women artists were again treated less favourably overall, receiving fewer, shorter commissions, less financial reward for their work, and enjoying less prestige and publicity. Only two women were given overseas commissions and only one, Evelyn Dunbar, was entrusted with a salaried position.

Post-war, the IWM has been the source of 'official' commissions, having established the Artistic Records Committee in 1972 to continue the tradition. It took a documentary approach, aiming to acquire historical records in an artistic form. More recently, in the context of changing artistic practice in contemporary art, the remit has changed. Renamed as the Art Commissions Committee in 2000, it now seeks to support artists to research and engage with conflict or post-conflict situations, and then to formulate a personal, artistic response. The opportunity to respond to modern conflicts continues to attract leading contemporary artists, both male and female. Of the fifty artists commissioned to date, twelve have been women (including two in male/female partnerships) representing approximately twenty-five per cent of the artists commissioned. Over the last decade the figure is over forty per cent, or three out of seven artists.

Outside official commissions, many female war artists have also worked independently, giving an unofficial view. This book takes an inclusive approach to war artists, encompassing those officially commissioned; artists working independently; artists for whom war or conflict are major themes; and those who have responded to conflict in particularly powerful individual works. This allows the expression of the unofficial artist – free to follow their own artistic and political agenda – to take its place alongside art supported by government patronage.

Artists working unofficially or on the fringes of official schemes, such as Paule Vézelay, Margaret Abbess, Priscilla Thornycroft and Pegaret Keeling offer a different perspective on wartime life. With the post-war reduction of government patronage for war art, it is essential to look outside the frame of official commissions to understand the breadth and range of artistic responses to war in contemporary art. Today, women artists engage with war through a whole range of approaches: investigating the fetishisation of weapons as in the work of Fiona Banner and Mona Hatoum; exploring memory and history like Susan Philipsz and Rozanne Hawksley; confronting horror and commemorating loss (Sophie Ristelhueber, Frauke Eigen and Rachel Whiteread); or teasing out complex personal, community and national identities as in the works of Rita Duffy, Sandra Johnston and Jananne Al-Ani.

The history of women as war artists mirrors the huge changes in society which have transformed expectations and opportunities for women in the last one hundred years. Social attitudes have restricted opportunities for women as artists, both in the past, and to a lesser extent today. Since the 1970s and 1980s feminist writers such as Griselda Pollock, Roszika Parker, and Germaine Greer have published research which uncovers and recovers the life and work of women artists, and explores why they have been excluded for so long from the established canons of art history. Much of this work has concentrated on artists from the Renaissance to the end of the nineteenth century, when women artists faced very evident and profound obstacles, such as lack of access to training.

Work has now begun on re-evaluating the work of women artists during the early and mid twentieth century. At this time women faced fewer social obstacles than in earlier periods, but had to confront a more subtle 'glass ceiling', arising from inequality of opportunity in exhibiting, commissioning, and critical evaluation.[3] The common approach of assessing and presenting modernism as a linear account of new movements and artistic groups has not served women artists well. A few outstandingly successful women artists have been included, but are seen as exceptional for their gender. Their inclusion serves to obscure a lack of recognition for the achievements of the greater body of women artists.[4]

Since the 1970s feminist artists such as American collective the Guerilla Girls – *Do women have to be naked to get into the Met. Museum?* – have campaigned actively for better access for women to the mechanisms of exhibition, market and critical evaluation.[5] However, even today the position for women artists is not comparable with the proportion of women in the population at large, and certainly not with the ratio of women studying art. Female students now account for about two-thirds of those studying fine art in the UK, and have been over half since the mid 1990s.[6] In 1998 women made up thirty-eight per cent of people in the UK whose main employment was as artists.[7] Only eleven per cent of artists in the Tate Collection are female, and their work comprises just seven per cent of the Collection.[8] Admittedly this in part reflects historic collecting practices which are difficult to redress retrospectively. A look at another indicator of artistic success, the Turner Prize, reveals that although thirty-nine out of eight-two (forty-eight per cent) of nominees have been women, only four (fifteen per cent) have ever won. There are signs of improvement here, however – only nineteen per cent of nominations were female from its beginning in 1984 until 1996, but between 1997 and 2010 forty-four per cent of nominees were women.

Women artists working today are aware of the work of feminist art historians and artists of the 1970s and 1980s, and are often very conscious of their identity and position as female artists. For some artists this has a direct impact on their practice, as they address gender issues, explore the female body, or examine women's experience. Others may work on themes which are unrelated to their gender, and yet the very fact that they are female may have significant implications for the way that their works will be understood and evaluated. Most would prefer not to be categorised or assessed as women artists, but simply as artists.

Women War Artists explores the remarkable experiences and achievements of a range of women war artists from the First World War to the present day, and shows the importance of women artists as eyewitnesses, participants, commentators and officially commissioned recorders of war. Examining their work, experiences and the artists' thoughts and reflections uncovers the unique opportunities and constraints they have encountered, and demonstrates the enormous diversity of their responses. Gathering the artists' work thematically – exploring their role in the war zone, looking at war work and gender on the home front and their approaches to the horror of war – reveals a great deal about social attitudes to women artists throughout this period.

[1] Sue Malvern, *Modern Art, Britain and the Great War, Witnessing, Testimony and Remembrance*, New Haven and London 2004, pp.181–6.

[2] Brian Foss, *War Paint: Art, War, State and Identity in Britain, 1939-1945*, London 2007, pp.196–204.

[3] Katy Deepwell, *Women Artists Between The Wars*, Manchester 2010, pp.5–6.

[4] Frances Borzello, *A World of Our Own – Women as Artists*, London 2000, pp.170–1.

[5] <http://www.guerillagirls.com/index.shtml> accessed 26 Nov. 2010.

[6] <http://www.hesa.ac.uk/dox/pubs_archive/student_03_04/tables/Table_2e.xls> accessed 25 Nov. 2010, <http://www.hesa.ac.uk/dox/pubs_archive/student_1994-95_table_2a.pdf> accessed 25 Nov. 2010.

[7] Gillian Feist, Andy Swanson and Trevor Jones, *Changing Landscapes: Women in Arts and Media Professions, European Comparisons, UK report*, London, ERICarts, Bonn (funded by European Commission and Arts Council England), 1999. p.196.

[8] Alicia Foster, *Guardian*, 7 April 2004. <http://www.guardian.co.uk/artanddesign/2004/apr/07/art.gender> accessed 25 Nov. 2010.

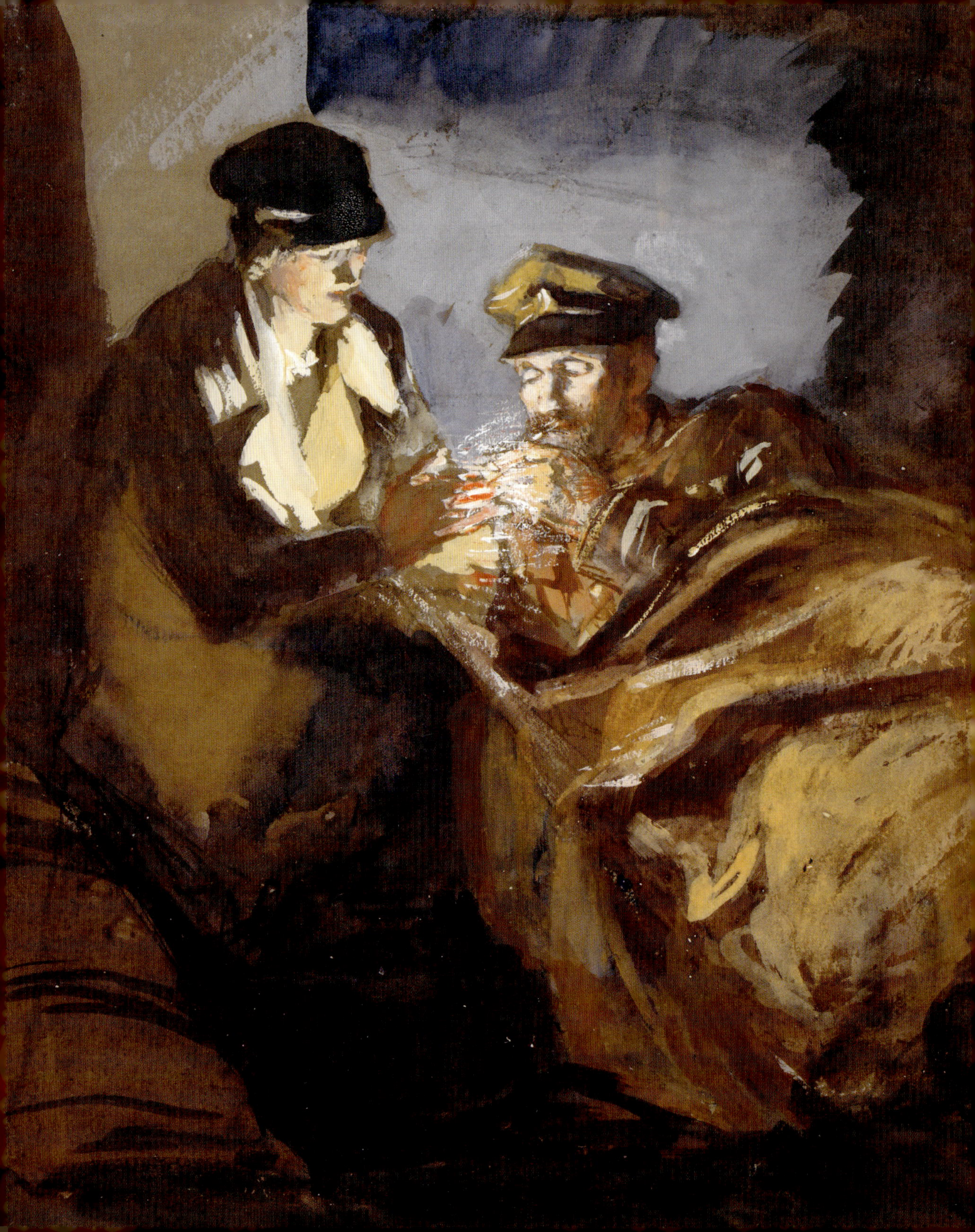

In the War Zone

For most of the twentieth century women artists had limited opportunities to encounter the realities of the front line, or to even enter the war zone. British government commissions to the theatres of war were few and far between. No women were commissioned to go to the front in the First World War, although the Imperial War Museum (IWM) acquired a small number of works after 1918. Two women were commissioned to go abroad to record the Second World War, but both travelled after the fighting had ended. It was not until 1982, when Linda Kitson was commissioned by the IWM to record the Falklands Conflict that a British female artist was sent overseas to accompany troops going into battle. Britain's Dominions and other allies similarly offered few official opportunities for women artists to access the front.

These restrictions on female artists are in line with attitudes towards female soldiers, which have slowly changed over the course of the twentieth century, but which continue to be an issue for debate today. Women were rather reluctantly accepted as auxiliaries in the services during the latter part of the First World War, in segregated units with limited roles. Ranks, badges and drills were all discouraged, although these military characteristics were present women's voluntary organisations such as the First Aid Nursing Yeomanry (FANY).[1] During the Second World War women again served in auxiliary units, and were not allowed to undertake combat roles. For example, although controversially they served in mixed anti-aircraft units, women were not allowed to fire the guns.[2] Notable exceptions were the female SOE (Special Operations Executive) agents, although even their duties were supposed to be 'non-combatant'. When Linda Kitson accompanied the task force to the Falklands, women were still not permitted to serve aboard naval vessels. Today women remain excluded from front line infantry roles in the British Army, although they are now accepted within the regular services.[3]

The First World War

Although no female artists were officially commissioned to enter the war zone, there were independent artists who found themselves close to the front line through medical work in hospitals and ambulance units. Olive Mudie-Cooke, already a trained artist, was working in France from 1916, driving ambulances for both FANY and subsequently the British Red Cross. This was at a time when celebrated soldier artists such as the Nash brothers and ambulance

Olive Mudie-Cooke

In an Ambulance: VAD Lighting a Cigarette for a Patient 1917–19

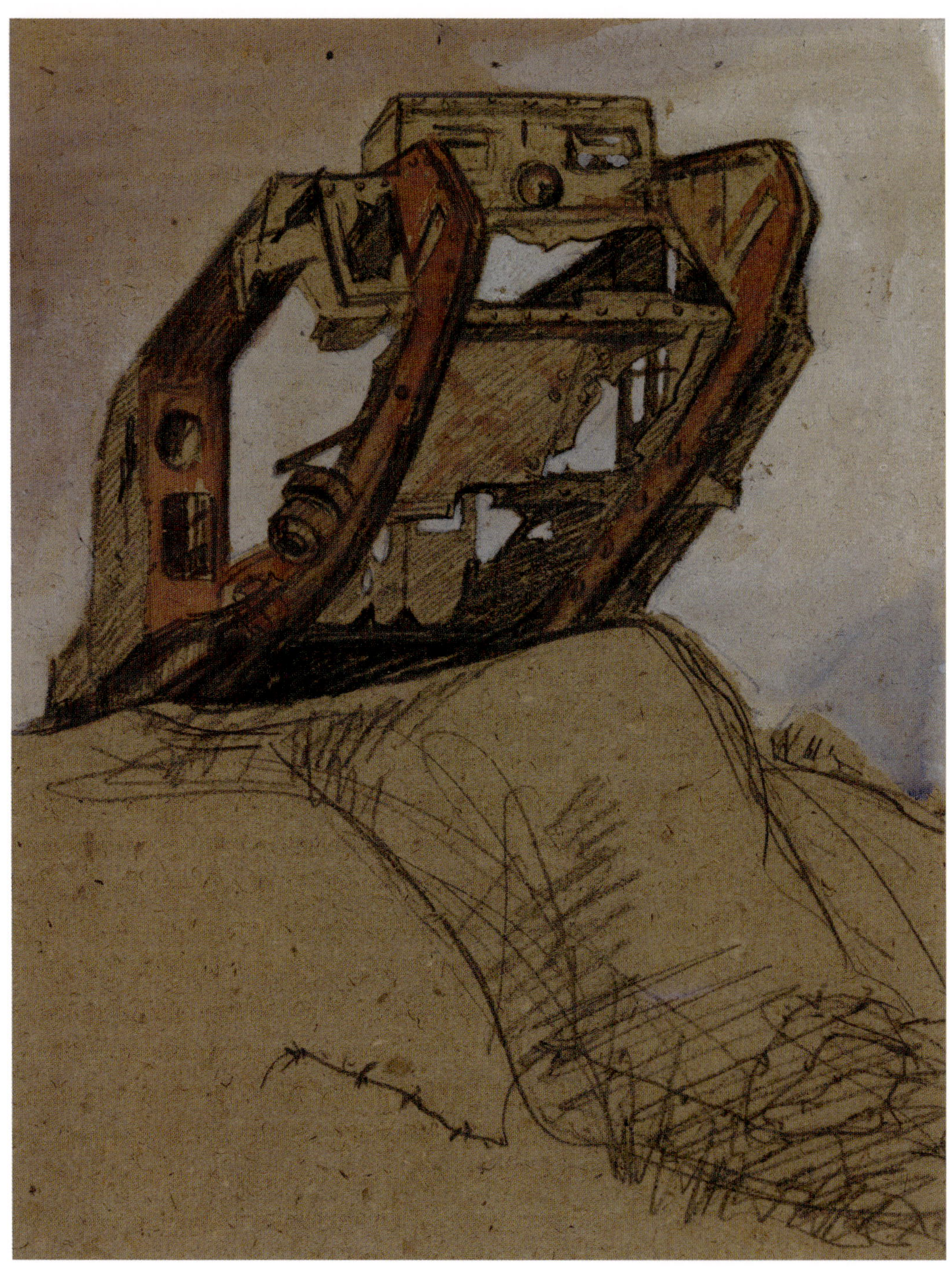

driver C.R.W. Nevinson were first making their mark in exhibitions at the Leicester Galleries. Mudie-Cooke's watercolours show the landscapes of the Somme and Italian front, and the work of medics behind the lines. She displays elegant draughtsmanship and a rich versatility, producing both the elegiac *Burnt Out Tank*, with its muted tones of rust, and the intensity and drama of *VAD Lighting a Cigarette for a Patient*.

Many of Mudie-Cooke's works now in the Collection of the IWM were acquired by the Women's Work Sub-committee (WWS) in 1919. This was one of several themed collecting groups established at this time to build the Museum's Collections. The WWS had strong links to the women's suffrage movement through its Chair, Lady Priscilla Norman, who was actively involved in the movement as Honorary Treasurer of the Liberal Women's Suffrage Union, and a member of the Executive Committee of the Women's Liberal Federation. She was also the wife of a liberal MP, Sir Henry Norman.[4] The focus of the WWS was recording the contributions of women during the war through all possible media, in support of the campaign to allow women to vote. Although they also acquired works by male artists, the WWS were very significant in bringing women artists into the IWM Collection, commissioning nine, as well as a female photographer and several female sculptors.[5]

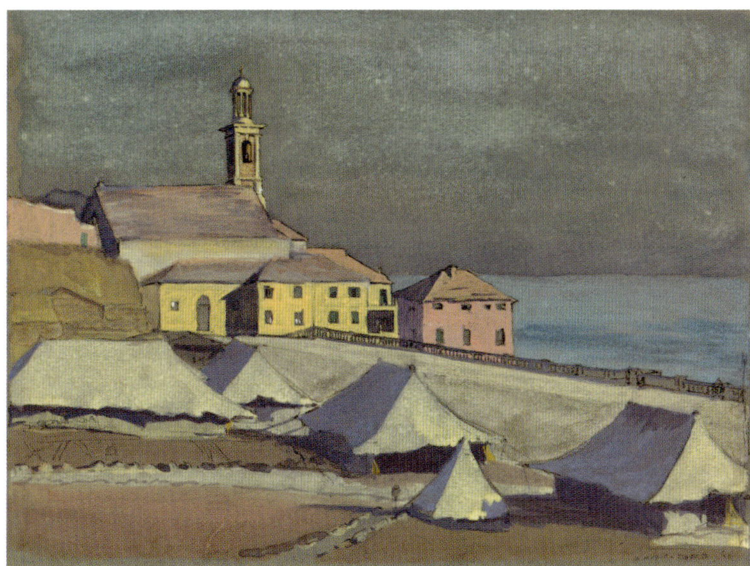

Olive Mudie-Cooke

Left: *Burnt Out Tank* 1917–19
Right: *'Con: Camp', Genoa* 1919

The photographer in question was Olive Edis, a successful studio portraitist, commissioned to record the many women who were still working in Belgium and France in medical and support roles of all kinds until late 1919. As an overseas visit, this was a very unusual commission. Edis travelled around the former war zone in a small contingent headed by Lady Norman herself, visiting and recording women's work of all kinds. The WWS clearly wished to supplement the official military photographic record – the results seem to place a greater emphasis on named women officers and women at work in a range of settings, not just those considered either novel or particularly suitable for women.

'I explained that the Imperial War Museum thought that a woman photographer, living among the girls in their camp, was likely to achieve more intimate pictures, more descriptive of their everyday life, than a man press photographer.'

In her wartime diary **Olive Edis** describes a conversation with Lieutenant Colonel A.N. Lee DSO, the official censor of art and photography.[6]

(Royal Photographic Society)

Olive Edis

Right: A member of Queen Mary's Army Auxiliary Corps welding at a Royal Air Force engine repair shop. Pont de l'Arche, France 1919

Below: The well-patronised French canteen at Sommesons, 1919

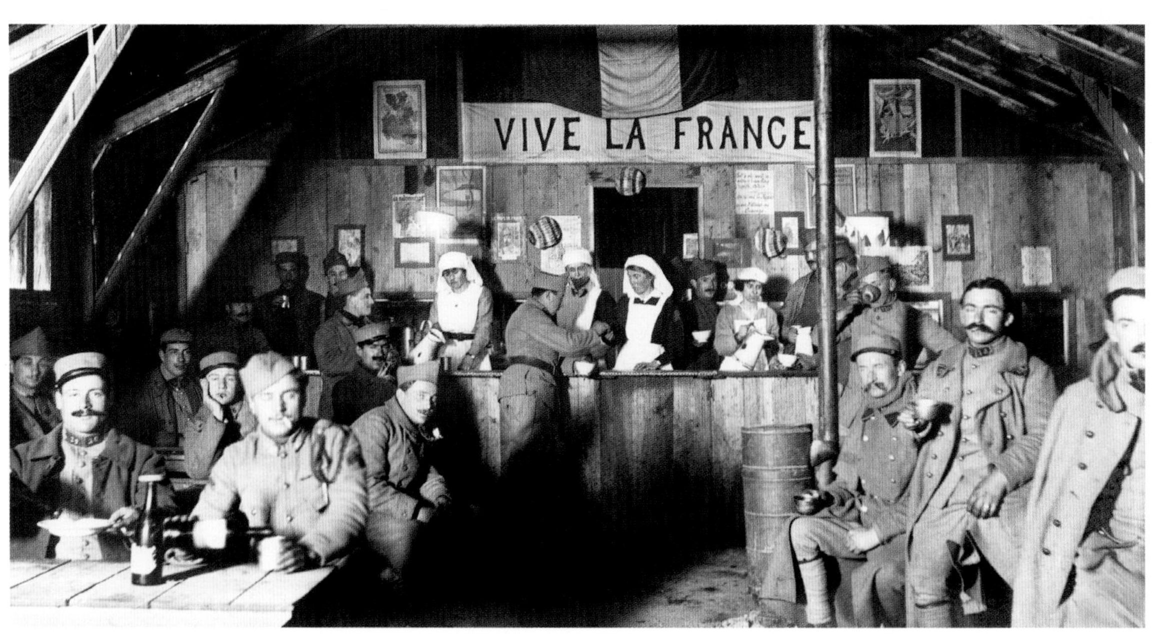

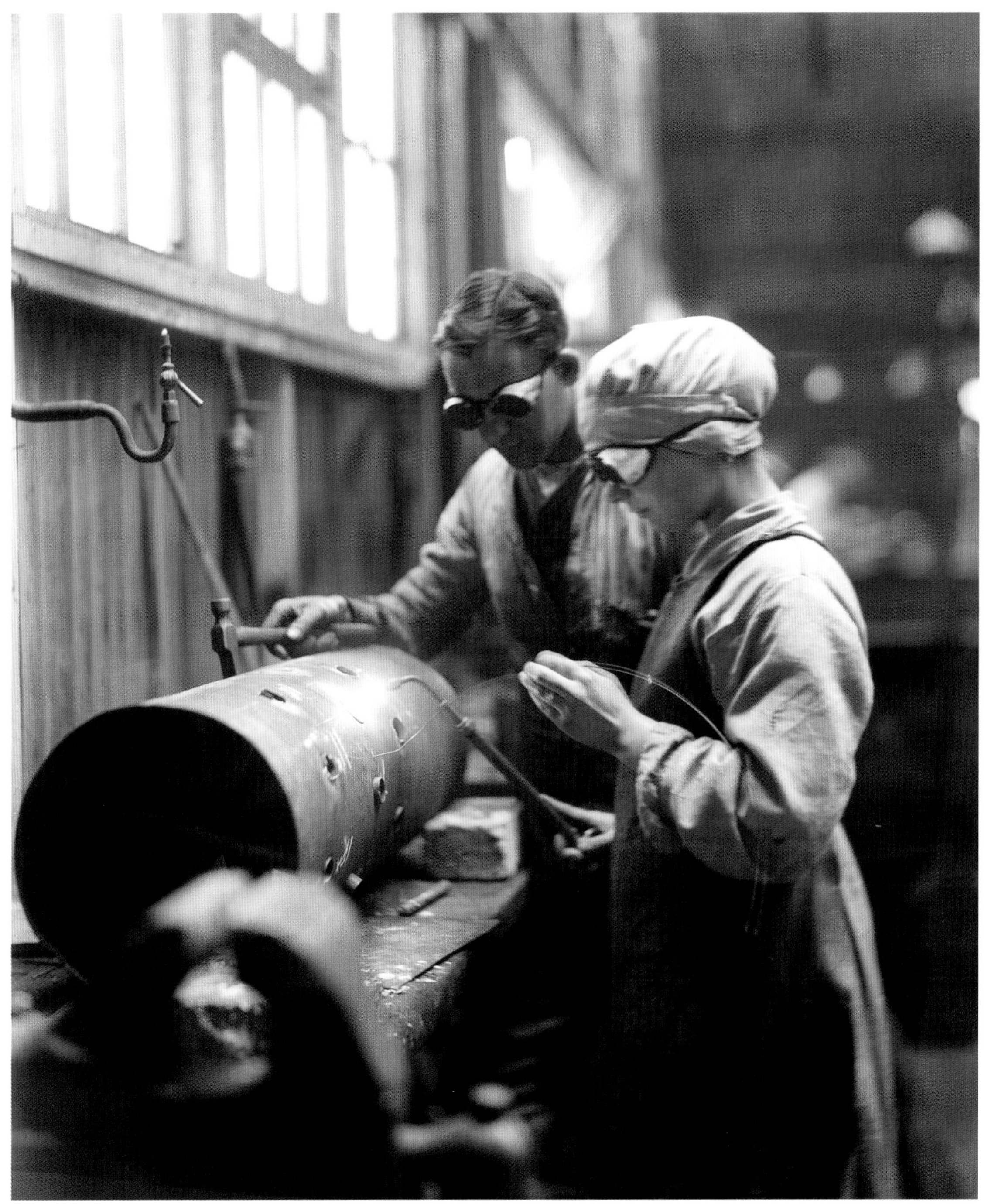

At this time a number of female artists including Elizabeth Butler, best known for her paintings of the Napoleonic and Crimean Wars, were also involved in creating battle paintings. These works were reconstructions of the dramatic events of battle, drawing on the tradition of history painting. It was, however, still relatively new for women artists to participate in this genre. Lucy Kemp-Welch specialised in showing horses in action during the Boer War and the First World War. The prestige and recognition she enjoyed in her lifetime is demonstrated by the purchase of *Forward the Guns!* for the Tate Gallery in 1917. It was important to Kemp-Welch to sketch outdoors from life; this painting was based on her direct observation of military exercises. Heroic battle paintings were still as popular as they had been in the nineteenth century. The government scheme, however, sought to collect artists at the forefront of an innovative, new war art which placed a strong emphasis on the artist as eye-witness. And so, like many male painters working in the tradition of battle painting, Kemp-Welch was not included, although the IWM later acquired work from her relating to the home front.

Lucy Kemp-Welch

Forward the Guns! 1917

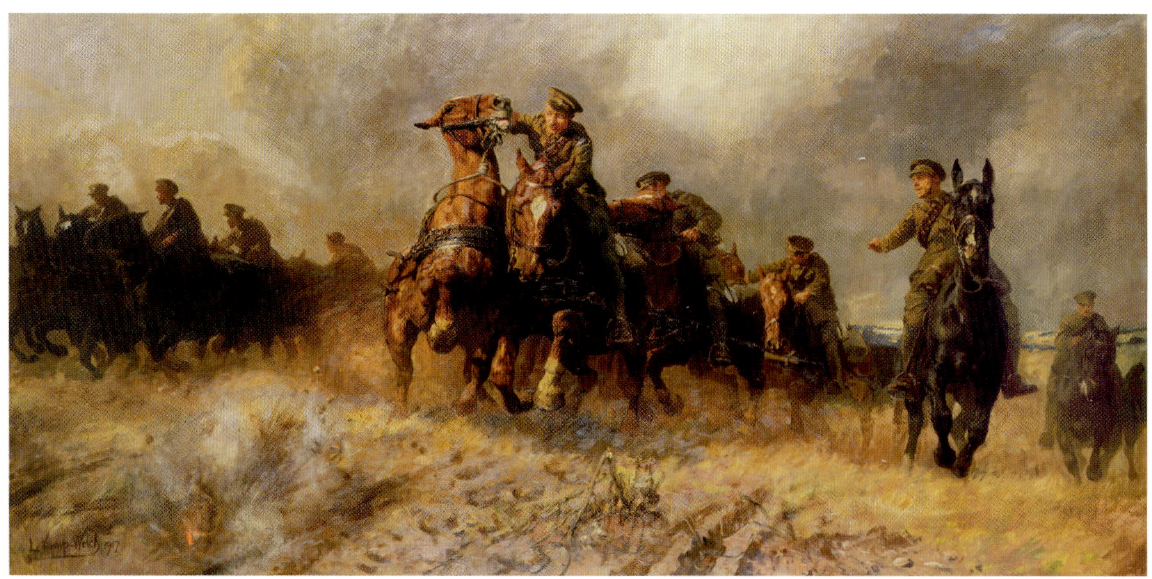

In 1945, as victory in Europe began to seem assured, Mary Kessell was preparing to go to Germany. She was one of only two women commissioned to go overseas by the War Artists Advisory Committee (WAAC – part of the British Ministry of Information) in contrast with the twenty-six men with overseas commissions.[7] By the time Kessell arrived in Germany the war was over, but she created memorable, intense drawings in charcoal and sanguine of homeless women and children in Berlin and destruction in Hamburg – both largely the result of Allied actions. Kessell also produced images of the slow renewal of life at Belsen resettlement camp, home to a range of refugees and displaced persons including some survivors of Bergen-Belsen concentration camp a few miles away.[8]

The second female artist to be given an overseas commission was Dame Laura Knight. Knight already enjoyed a very high level of prestige and recognition as the first female artist since 1768 to become a full member of the Royal Academy (RA). She painted with a bold, muscular realism, and was well known for her appealing portrayals of circus and dance performers. Her status enabled her to request an overseas commission – to paint the war crimes trials before the International Military Tribunal at Nuremberg. Knight's painting *The Nuremberg Trial* is quite different from the portraits she had created for the WAAC to meet a wartime propaganda need for heroes and role models. It seems clear that the subject and the experience moved her, and challenged her into a departure from her usual realist style.

Other women artists working independently were also present in the war zone during the Second World War, and in some cases their work was then purchased by the WAAC. The British Red Cross commissioned Doris Zinkeisen to portray their work in Europe. Her strongest contribution was her searing images from the liberation of Bergen-Belsen concentration camp, later acquired for the WAAC because of their importance (see 'The Costs of War'). Stella Schmolle joined the Auxiliary Territorial Service (ATS) in late 1941, serving as a draughtswoman first in camouflage, but later in intelligence. The WAAC assisted her with obtaining facilities and support from her Commanding Officers to record the work of the ATS. They subsequently purchased a series of paintings and drawings covering her training and service in England, Belgium and France from 1941–5. Schmolle shows her comrades in a wide range of different activities at home and abroad – some of her best works capture telling details of the rigours of civilian and army life in newly-liberated Europe.

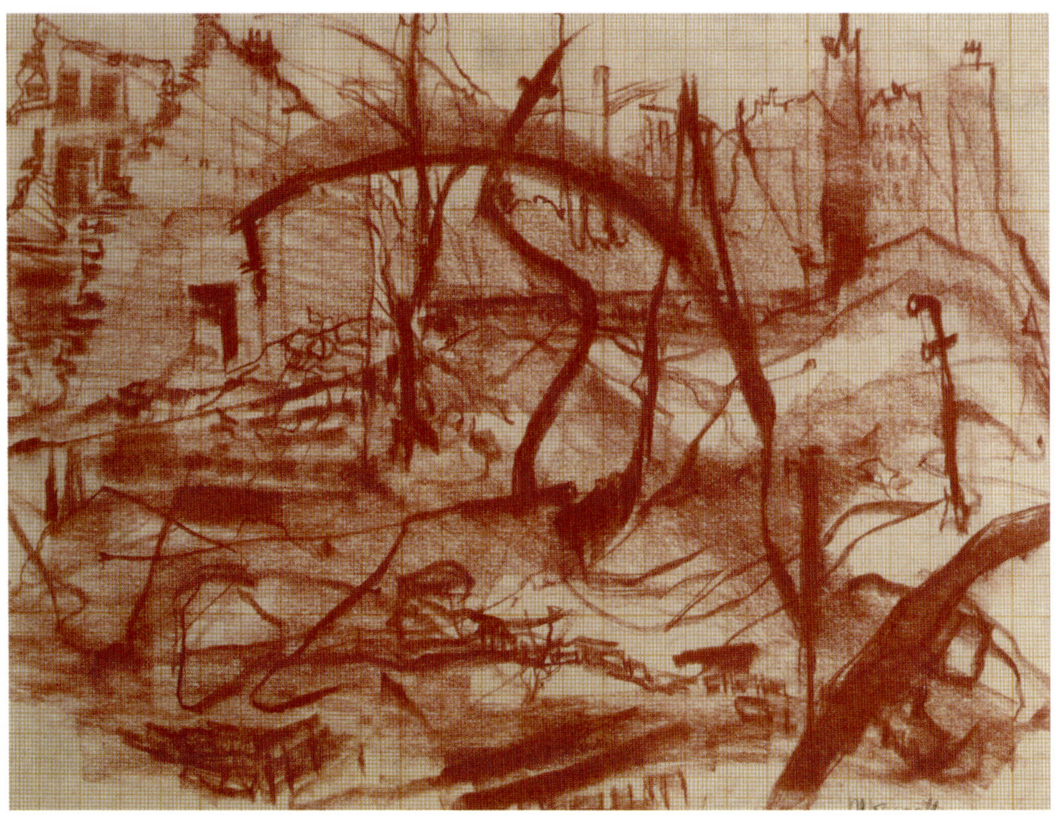

Mary Kessell

Above: *Ruins in Hamburg:
The Dock Area* 1945

Right: *Waiting for the Train on
the Anhalter Bahnhof, Berlin,
December 1945* 1945

Below right: *Two Children
at a Berlin Railway Station,
Germany 1945* 1945

'The brown blasted bridges, the pink, red and black
ruins … against the cloudy angry sky. The sun
that was trying to shine and the utter devastation,
street upon street, back – way back, and the colour
of it all. The twisted gateways – the broken statues –
the shells of churches and the river – stilled in its
business – packed tight with ships and more iron
and twisted girders.'

Mary Kessell's diary entry recording her impressions of
the devastated city of Hamburg, September 1945.

(Imperial War Museum Documents and Sound Section)

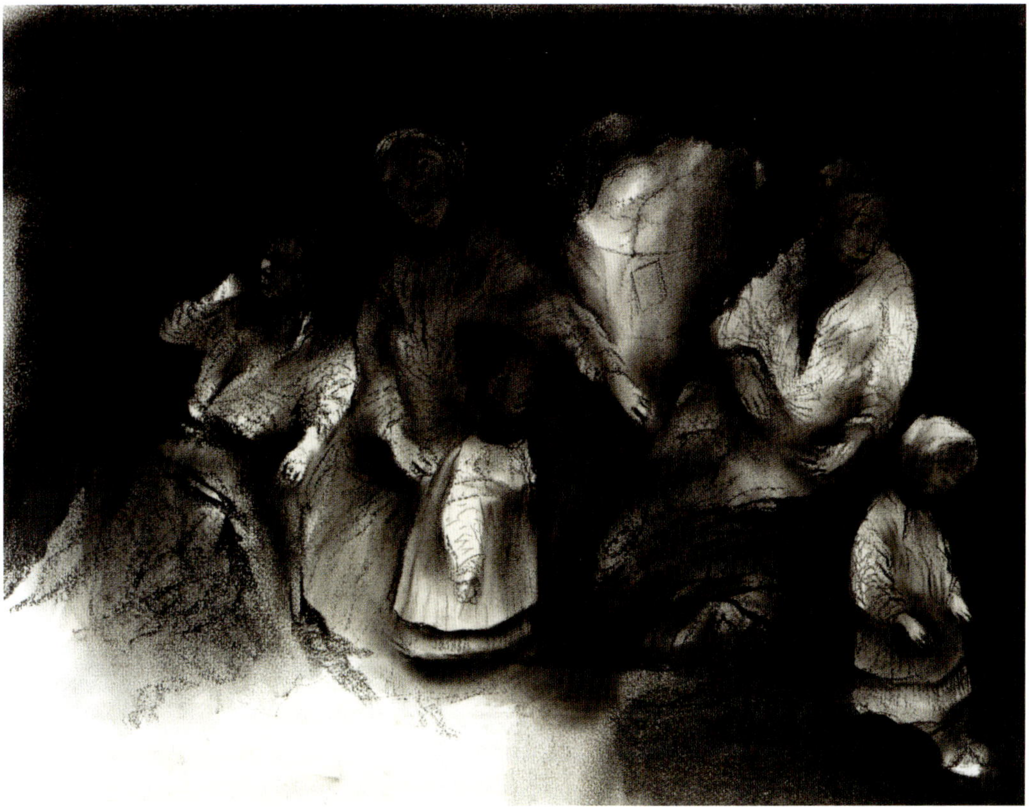

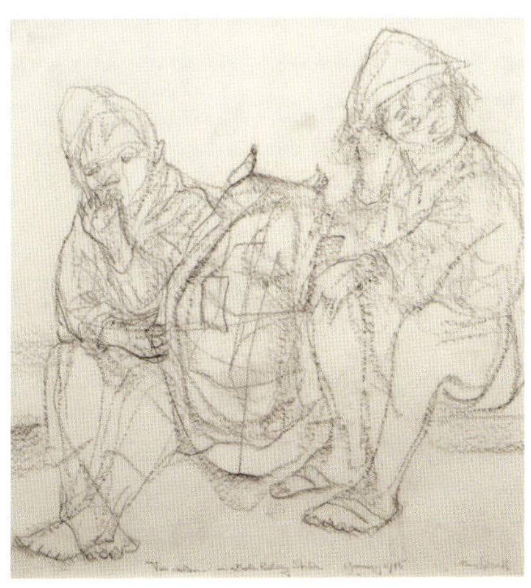

'Will they ever live again? These bits and pieces of dirt and rags – shuffling – crawling – dribbling. These apathetic bundles of rags staring into space – waiting for trains that never came.'

Mary Kessell's diary entry describing refugees she saw at a Berlin railway station during her September 1945 visit to the city.

(Imperial War Museum Documents and Sound Section)

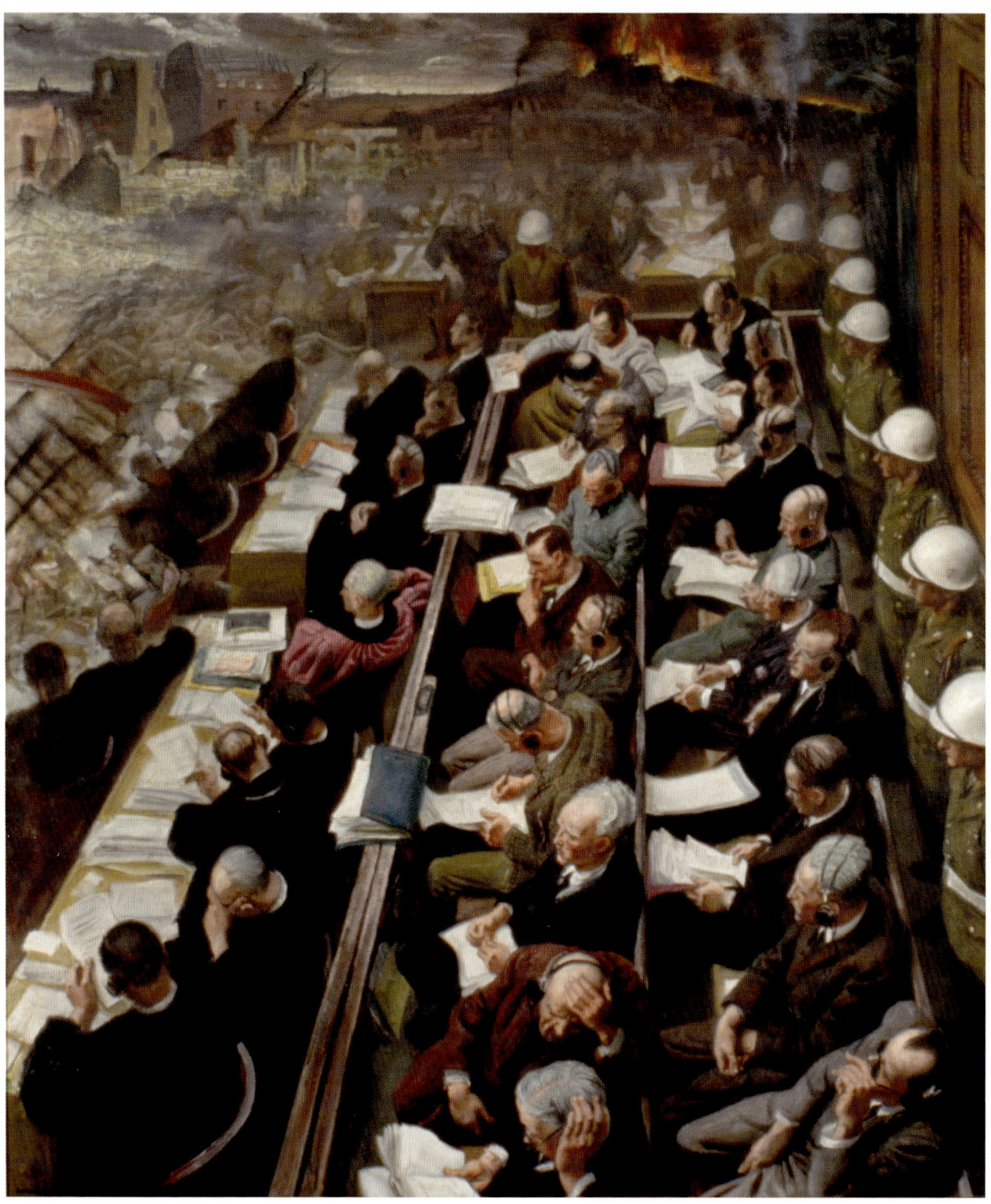

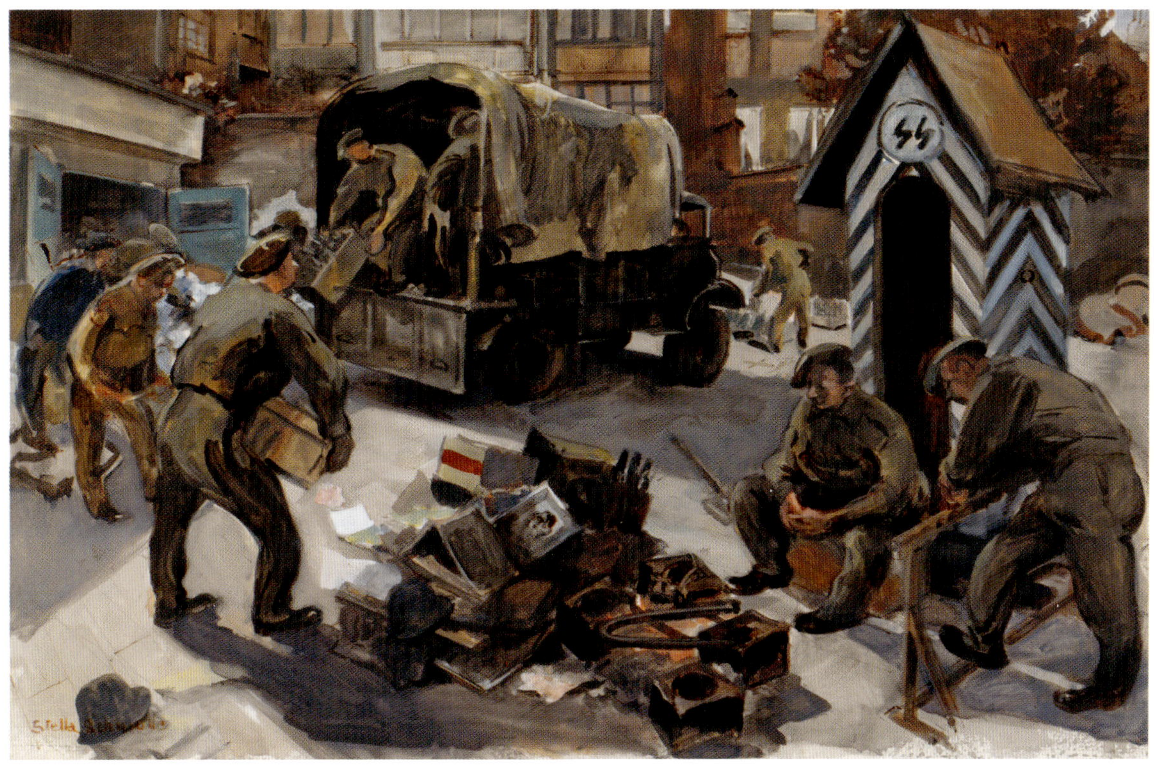

Laura Knight

Left: *The Nuremberg Trial* 1946

'In that ruined city death and destruction are ever present. **They** had to come into the picture, without them, it would not be the Nuremburg as it now is during the trial, when the death of millions and utter devastation are the sole topic of conversation wherever one goes – whatever one is doing.'

In a letter to the War Artists Advisory Committee, **Laura Knight** explains the unusual composition of her painting, *The Nuremberg Trial*.

(Imperial War Museum War Artists Archive)

Stella Schmolle

Above: *Pioneers Clearing Out an SS HQ Brussels October 1944* 1944

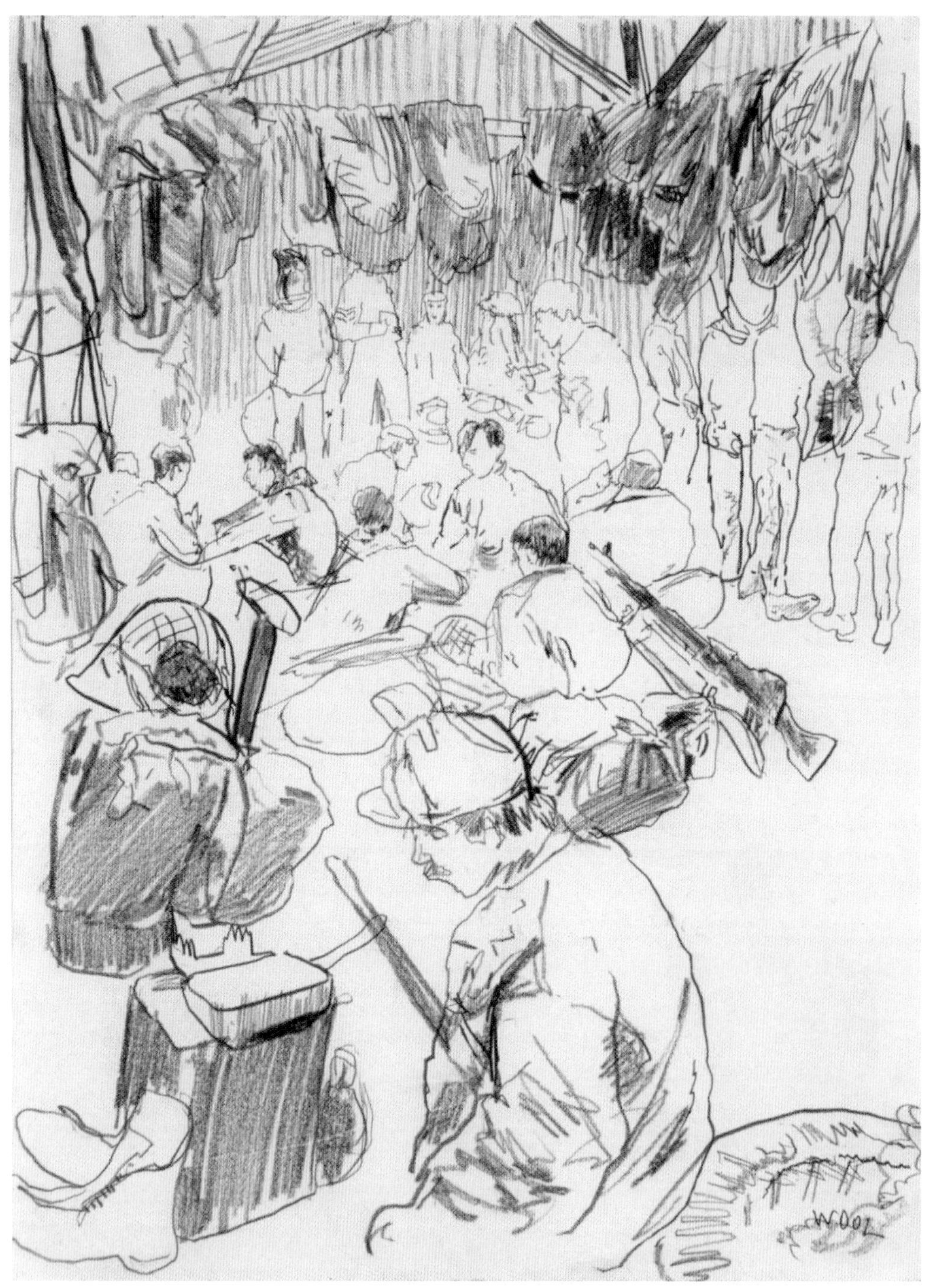

Post-war and Contemporary

The post-war era saw a changed mode of warfare typified by smaller, post-colonial conflicts. During the stand-off of the Cold War these were often a form of 'war by proxy' between the Soviet Union and the United States. This kind of conflict did not have the same kind of immediacy of impact, or indeed enjoy the same degree of unquestioning support from the populations of the UK or the US. Official war art commissions in the UK were in abeyance until the early 1970s, when the Imperial War Museum (IWM) began to commission artists once again, initially to record in artistic form the involvement of British troops in Northern Ireland. Yet very few of these commissions were awarded to women artists, and those that were served mainly to record the peacetime activities of women in the armed forces.

In 1982, however, Argentina invaded the Falkland Islands and Linda Kitson was commissioned to accompany the Task Force that sailed to regain them. This was a huge milestone, and her commission attracted enormous media interest, much of it relating to her gender. Linda Kitson's family connections in defence and the military, together with her skill in rapid reportage drawing much in the tradition of WAAC artists such as Bawden and Gross, made her very acceptable to the Ministry of Defence (MOD). Even so, the original intention for her commission was that she disembark at Ascension Island and go no further. Instead she continued to accompany the troops throughout the campaign, and despite the rigours of the conditions, produced drawings of deceptive simplicity and great skill. These capture many of the incongruities of the conflict and, in the absence of much independent media coverage, form an important record of the events.

More recently, in 2002 the Imperial War Museum commissioned Nikki Bell and Ben Langlands to create work in response to the end of the first phase of conflict in Afghanistan – then regarded optimistically as the start of a process of nation-building. Together they made a series of works recorded in their book, *The House of Osama Bin Laden* (also the title of their 2003 exhibition, and one of the pieces in it). The diary of Langlands and Bell's 2002 research visit to Afghanistan reveals the remarkably robust, courageous and practical way in which they approached the task, and gives glimpses of the particular quality of Nikki Bell's experience.

Outside of these official commissions, many women artists have visited or inhabited war zones since the Second World War. Opportunities have increased for women, and female war

Linda Kitson

2nd Battalion Scots Guards in the Sheep Sheds at Fitzroy, 17 June 1982
1982

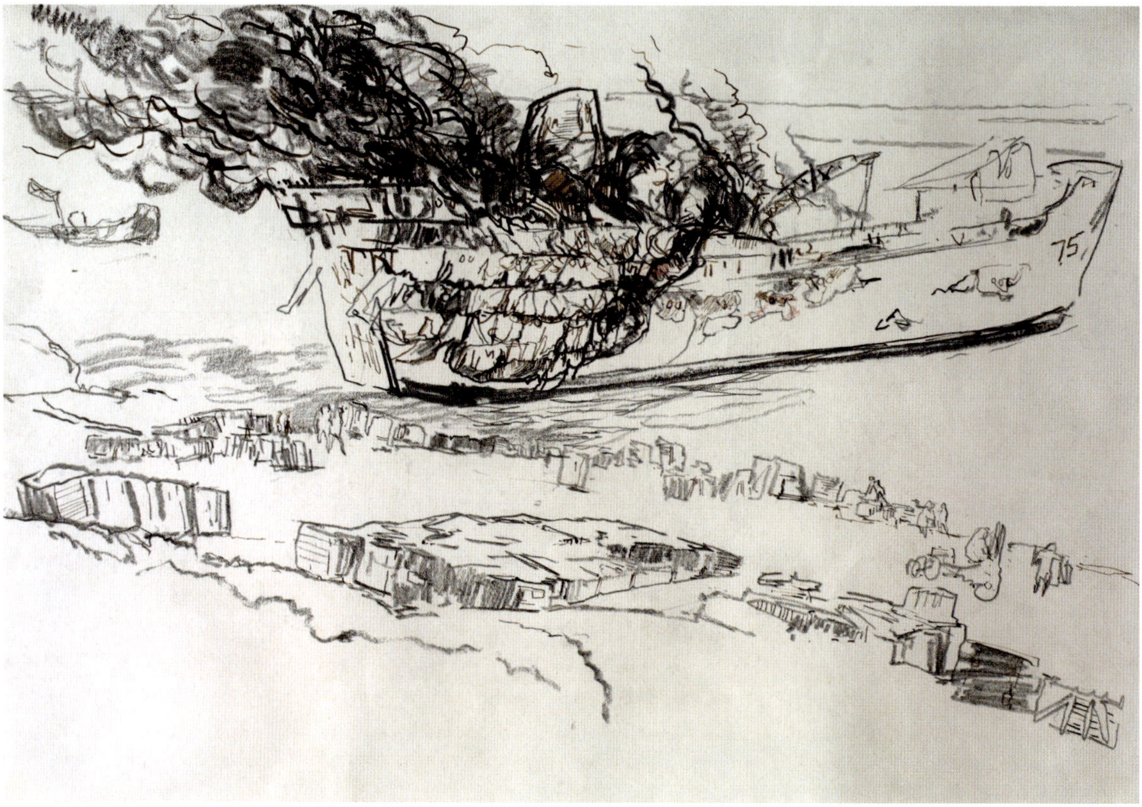

Linda Kitson

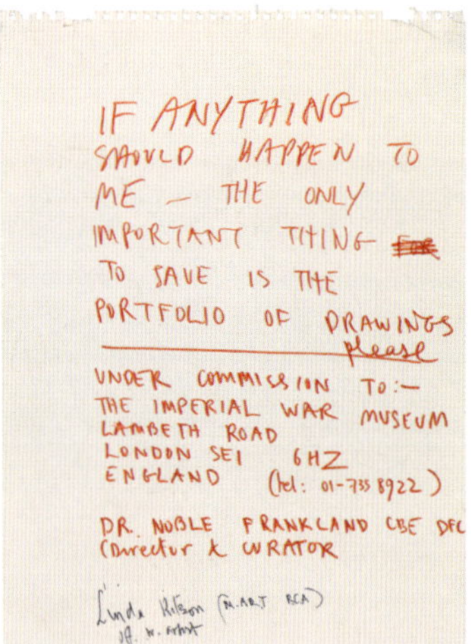

Above: *Sir Galahad Moored at Fitzroy. She continued
to burn until she was towed out to sea and sunk as
a war grave. 16 June 1982* 1982

Left: *'The only important thing to save is the portfolio
of drawings please...'* 1982

photographers have become more common. The line between documentary photography and fine art has become increasingly blurred – it is in this delicate border area that Sophie Ristelhueber operates. Ristelhueber was a pioneer in the development of a new artistic approach to photography, in sharp contrast to the photojournalistic genre of images of war victims so strong during the Vietnam War and beyond. She often focuses on landscape and architecture, using these as a metaphor for individual suffering, and as a means of capturing a collective, societal impact. There is also the Postmodernist's awareness and willingness to quote from earlier artists, and it is interesting to compare Ristelhueber's *Iraq 2001* with Paul Nash's seminal *We Are Making a New World*, 1918.

In Northern Ireland's complex experience of contemporary conflict there is no 'war zone' as such, but rather many contested spaces intermingling with everyday life. Mary McIntyre's *Veil 1* depicts a landscape redolent of complex and contradictory meanings. This opaque view seems to embody an unknown future: signs of new development and the 'peace dividend', but also the fragility of peace in hard economic times. Decontextualised by the fog, the landscape could be a building site, or a burial site. The sense of powerful forces at work draws on the concept of the sublime, also evoked by an earlier generation of artists engaging with the First World War.

[1] Lucy Noakes, *Women in the British Army: War and the Gentle Sex, 1907–48*, London 2006, pp.39–81.

[2] Brian Foss, *War Paint: Art, War, State and Identity in Britain, 1939–1945*, London 2007, p.152.

[3] Noakes, *Women in the British Army*, pp.x–xii.

[4] Mary Wilkinson, 'Members of The Women's Work Subcommittee', *Women, Work and Society 1914–1918*, Cengage resource based on the Women's Work Collection at the IWM. <http://www.tlemea.com/Resources.asp#committee> accessed 12 Nov. 2010.

[5] Katy Deepwell, 'Women War Artists of World War One', *Women's Contributions to Visual Culture 1918–1939*, 2008. The sculpture artists, to whom Deepwell draws attention, made models of women's war work, some of which have been retained in the Exhibits section of the IWM's Collection.

[6] Jane Carmichael, 'Olive Edis: Imperial War Museum Photographer in France and Belgium, March 1919', *Imperial War Museum Review*, no.4, 1989, pp.4–11.

[7] Nineteen male artists were given full time salaried commissions overseas, including some who were released from active duty for this purpose. Of the seven given short-term contracts, three were serving soldiers already abroad.

[8] Ulrike Smalley, 'Objective realists – British War Artists as Witnesses to the Liberation of Bergen-Belsen Concentration Camp', *The Holocaust in History and Memory*, vol. 2, 2009, pp.53–67.

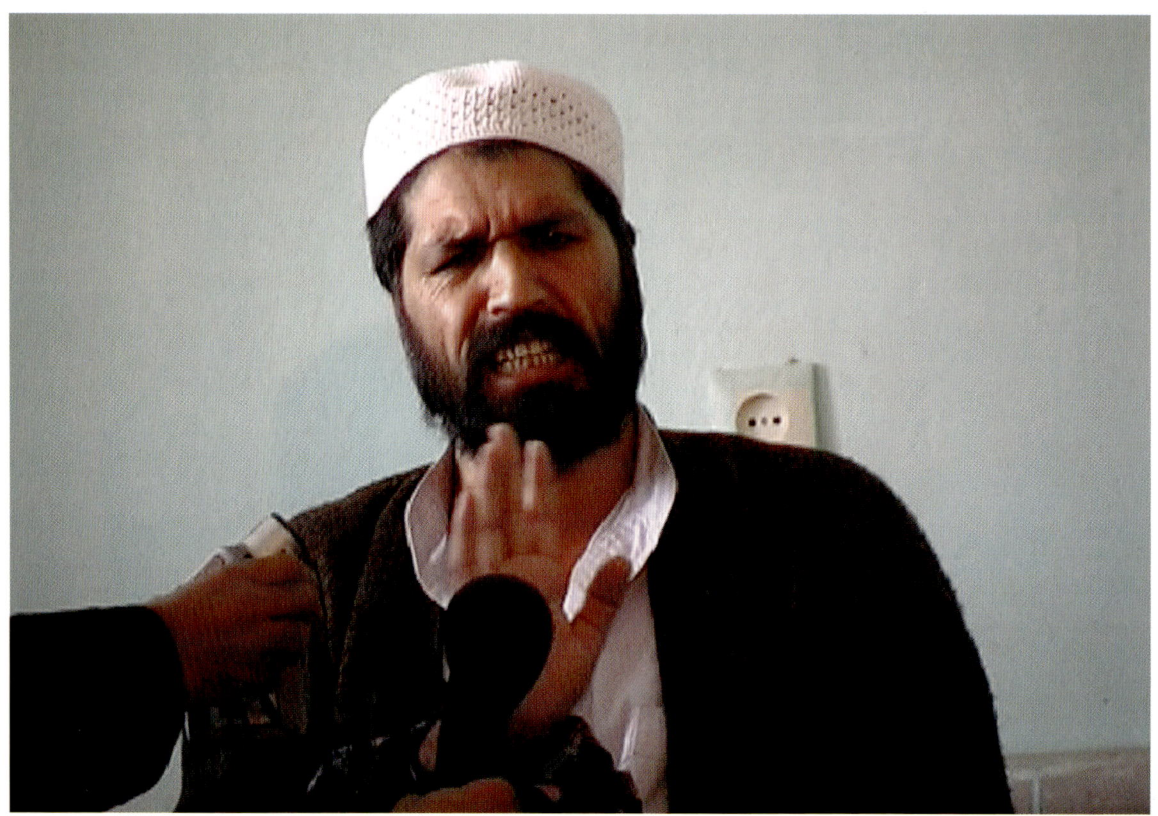

Langlands & Bell

Zardad's Dog [Film Still] 2003

'Tuesday 15 10 02

While we wait for the trial to begin, we are introduced to
a mullah who is a judge. He shakes hands with Nikki and
laughs, saying that he never normally shakes
hands with a woman.'

Extract from 'Afghan Diary' in *The House of Osama Bin Laden* by **Langlands & Bell**, recording the
duo's research visit and the events leading up to the filming for *Zardad's Dog*.

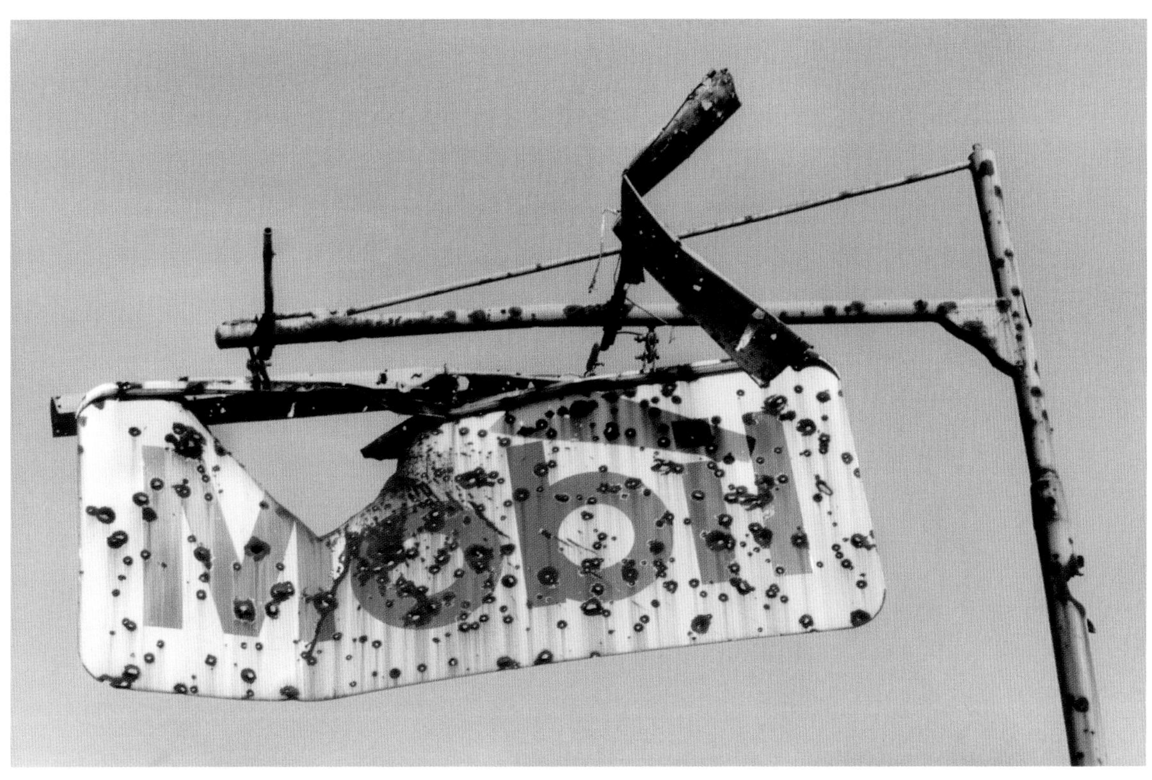

Sophie Ristelhueber

Beirut, photographs 1984

Black and white photograph, silver print.
50 x 60cm © Sophie Ristelhueber / adagp Paris

'Looking back through the 1980s I saw that, although it's
not my only interest, I kept a lot of my focus on traces, scars,
and so on. The first time you can see that is in my Beirut
work from 1982 about modern architecture in ruins.'

Sophie Ristelhueber, in a 2009 interview with Guy Lane for *Art World* magazine, reflects on the underlying
theme of scars, both in landscape and body, which emerges on looking back at her work.

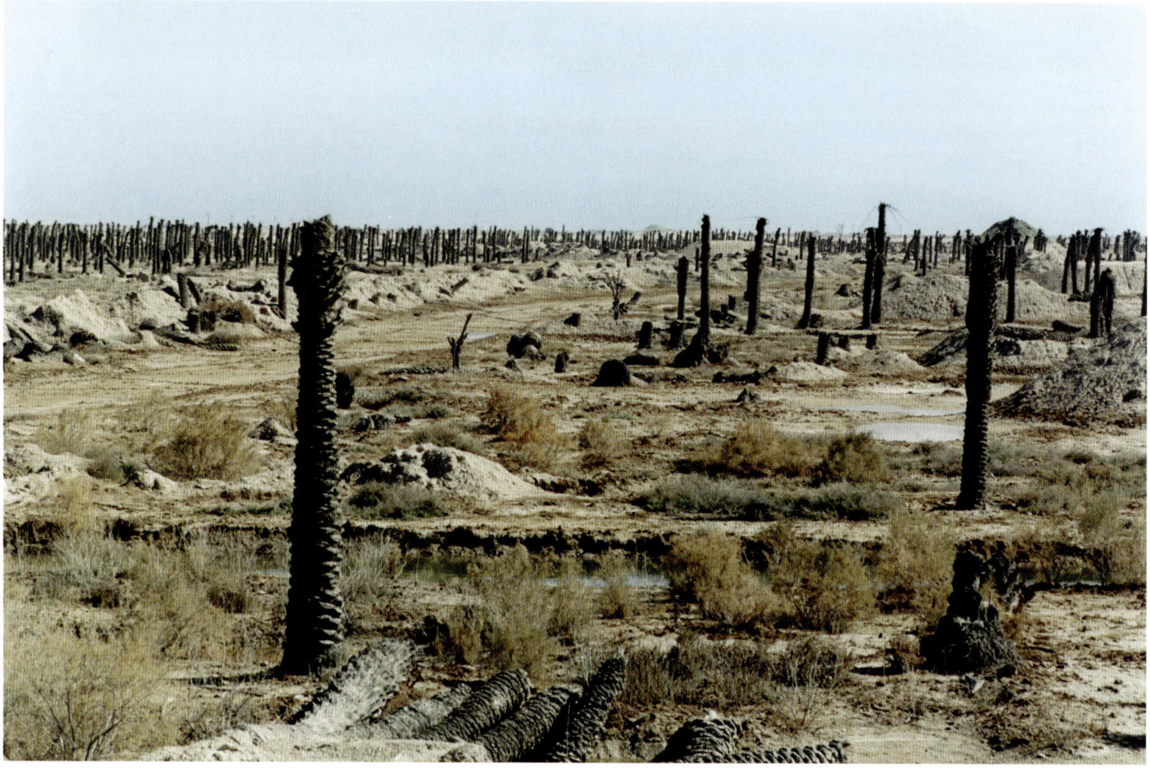

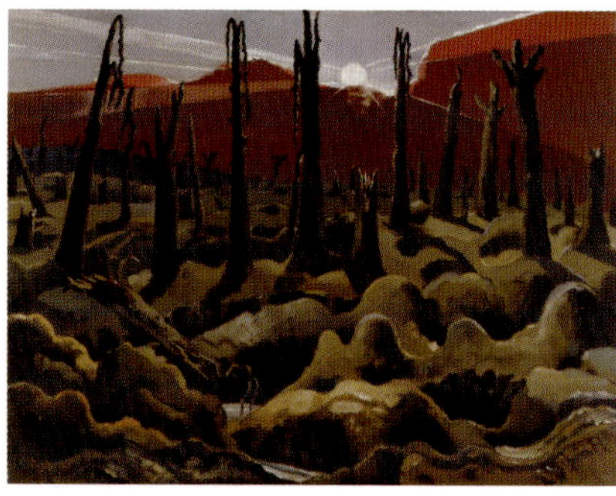

Sophie Ristelhueber

Above: *Iraq* [Part of a triptych] 2001

Colour photograph, chromogenic print mounted on aluminium.
120 x 180cm. © Sophie Ristelhueber / adagp Paris

Left: Paul Nash
We Are Making a New World 1918

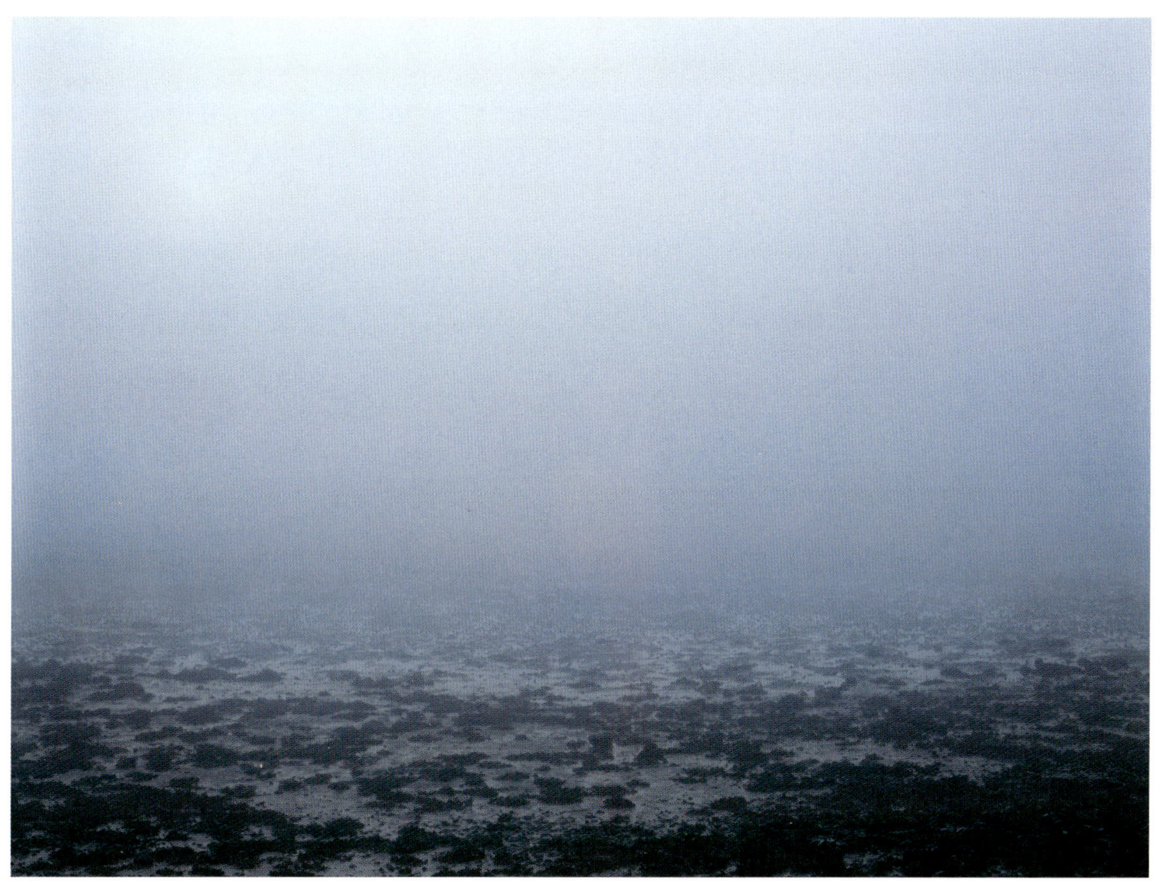

Mary McIntyre

Veil 1 2006
Colour Lightjet Photograph Print

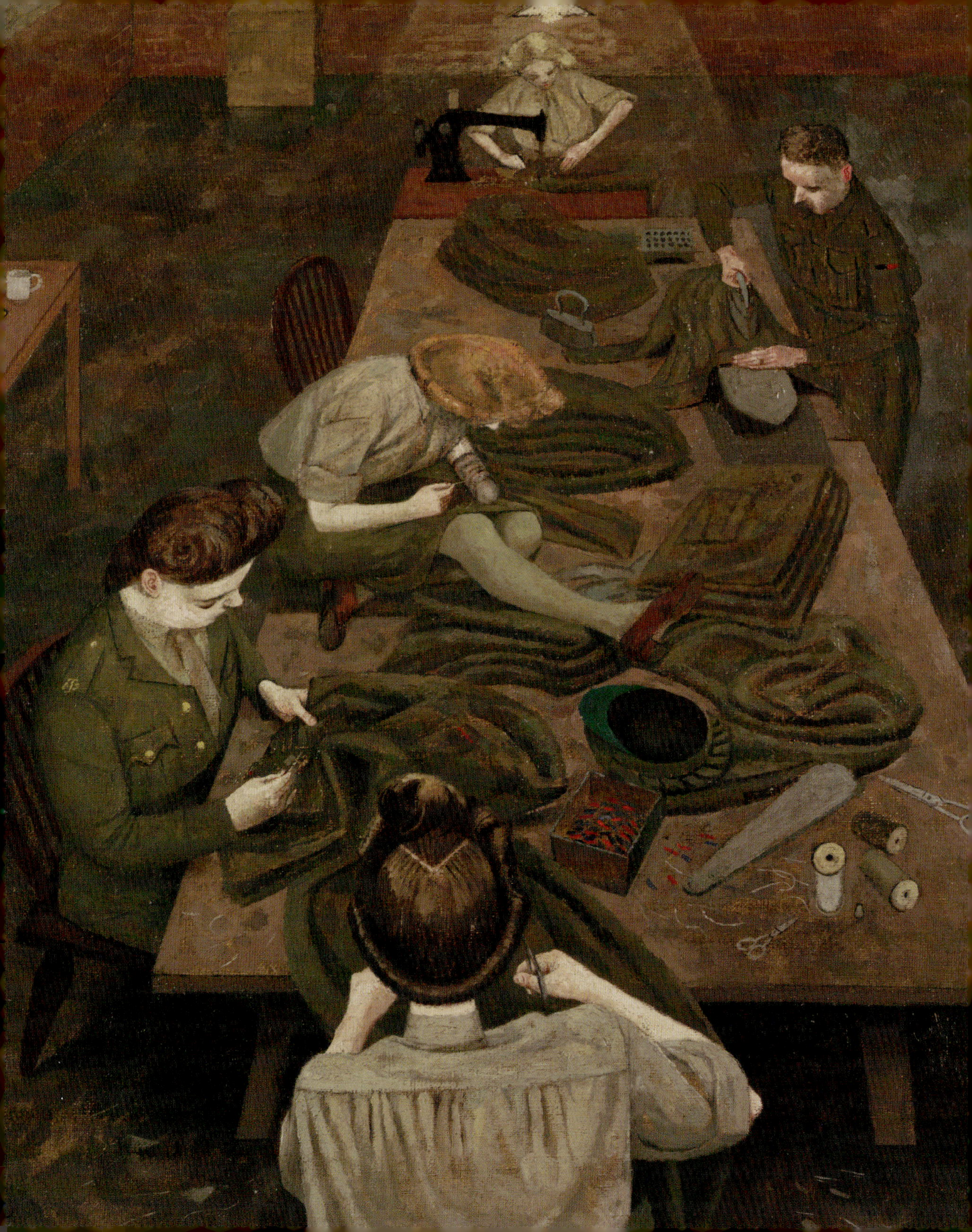

Working Together

It was not until late in the First World War that the focus of British government war art commissioning shifted from military effort to the involvement of British society as a whole in supporting the war effort. Consequently the home front found fuller artistic expression within the nascent Imperial War Museum (IWM), established by the War Cabinet in 1917. The vast majority of official commissions for women artists in the First World War came from the IWM's Women's Work Sub-committee (WWS) rather than the Ministry of Information (MOI)'s war artists schemes, which almost entirely excluded women. This origin determined the nature and scope of the commissions, focussed on women's wartime roles rather than any broader themes.

In contrast, the majority of all official commissions from the government's War Artists Advisory Committee (WAAC) during the Second World War (for men and women) were on home front subjects. This was due to Britain's beleaguered situation in the early part of the war, but continued as a means of retaining public support for total war. Once again commissions for women artists were largely directed towards women's war work or traditionally female concerns.

Since the Second World War artists have responded to changing patterns of conflict in diverse ways, driven by their own personal, political and creative agendas. Post-war, and certainly following the burgeoning of feminism in the 1970s, contemporary female artists have explored gender roles and women's experiences in present and past conflicts. The choice of artistic media such as textile and performance has become politicised as part of a struggle for female artistic recognition.

Women Employed in 'Men's Work'

In officially commissioned works from both World Wars there is a strong emphasis on women occupying traditionally male roles. It was in proving themselves adequate substitutes for men that women's contributions to the war effort were most valued, and yet most discomforting to society.

By the end of the First World War almost two million additional women had been encouraged into employment in a wide range of jobs, mainly outside of the services, in order to release men for combat.[1] For a brief period after the war women's contributions were widely acknowledged. The WWS was keen to capitalise on the national mood, using women's war work to back the cause of votes

Evelyn Dunbar

*An Army Tailor and
an ATS Tailoress* 1943

for women. In 1918 some women were indeed given the vote for the first time, and universal suffrage for women would come in 1928. However, there was also a backlash – it was not long before women workers were deprived of their jobs for fear of high unemployment amongst returning male veterans.

The WWS chose artists on its own terms, and often circumvented the advice and preferences of the IWM's Art Sub-committee. Victoria Monkhouse was identified for a commission through a network of female contacts based around Cambridge University. Her images have a softness which serves both to emphasise the gender of her subjects and to underplay the departure from social conventions as they carry out their duties as bus conductors, post women or window cleaners.

Women were also portrayed in more active, physically demanding and even dangerous work. Lucy Kemp-Welch, the well-known illustrator of the children's classic *Black Beauty*, demonstrated her expertise in painting horses and strong, vigorous women in two large paintings, *The Straw Ride* and *The Ladies' Army Remount Depôt, Russley Park Wiltshire*. Women were employed in training and caring for war horses from as early as 1915, and Russley Park was the largest depot of its kind to be staffed entirely by women. In Anna Airy's *Women Working in a Gas Retort House: South Metropolitan Gas Company, London*, women are employed in the creation of coal gas, or 'town' gas. Although the heaviest parts of this work were mechanised, it was still dirty and dangerous.

Lucy Kemp-Welch

Right: *The Straw Ride: Russley Park Remount Depôt, Wiltshire* 1919–20

Anna Airy

Below right: *Women Working in a Gas Retort House: South Metropolitan Gas Company, London* 1918

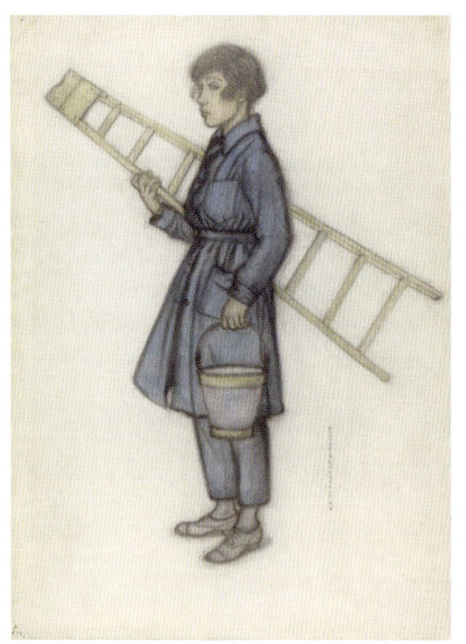

Victoria Monkhouse

Left: *A Woman Window-Cleaner* 1919

'I will let you have them as soon as possible. I hope however you will be able to give me sufficient time to do the work satisfactorily. Women workers are so busy that sittings often have to be rather far between, otherwise there would be no difficulty in getting the work finished quickly.'

In a letter to the Imperial War Museum in November 1918, Victoria Monkhouse explains why her drawings of women war workers are taking longer to complete than expected.

(Imperial War Museum War Artists Archive)

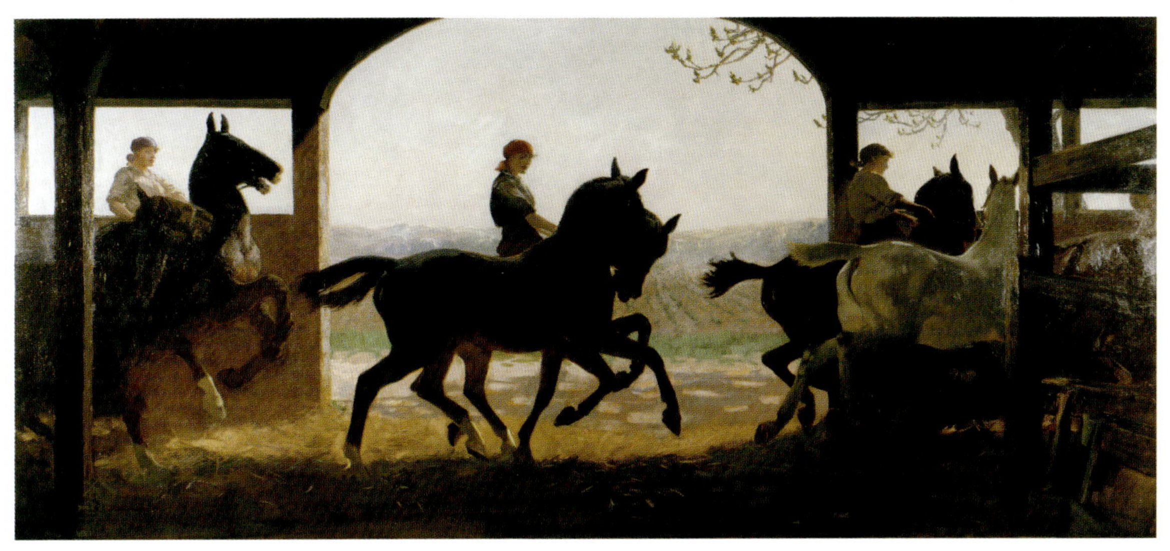

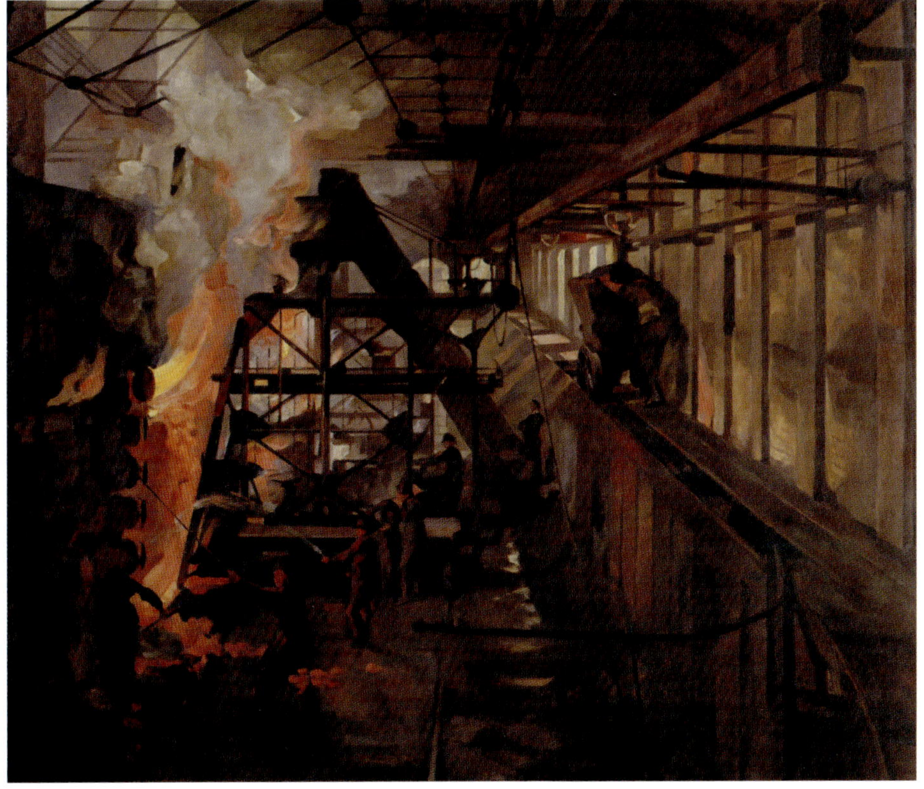

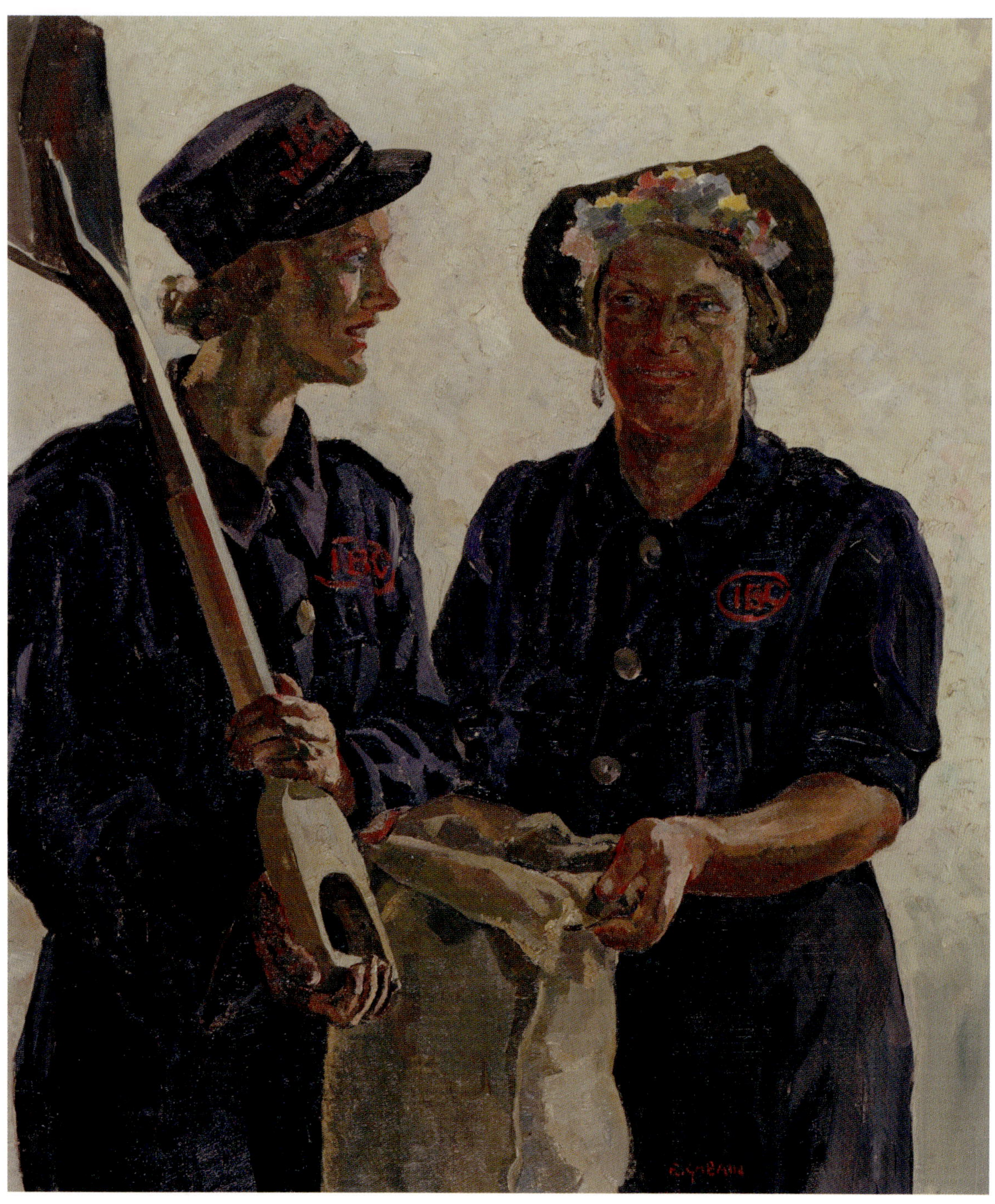

During the Second World War women again played a hugely significant role as auxiliaries in the services, working in wartime industry and in administrative and caring positions. The recruitment of women was slower than hoped for in the early years of the war. Propaganda efforts were therefore directed towards promoting women's work, before the gradual introduction of conscription for women from December 1941.

Like its First World War forerunners, Ethel Gabain's painting *Sandbag Filling, Islington Borough Council* shows anonymous female war workers involved in hard physical labour as council employees. Gabain received a range of commissions from the WAAC. A renowned printmaker, she was also asked to make a series of lithographs of women in industry, medicine and agriculture.

Stella Schmolle was conscripted into the Auxiliary Territorial Service (ATS), and recorded many aspects of its work for the WAAC. Her watercolour *The Dough Room: Aldershot Command Bakery* shows women baking – a domestic activity transformed into an industrial one. Others show women training in new skills, including vehicle maintenance, and in all these images women appear confident, energetic and eager to learn.

Discomfort with the new roles of women manifested itself – as it had during the First World War – in scurrilous rumours of both promiscuity and lesbianism amongst servicewomen, centred on the ATS.[2] This can be seen reflected humorously in some of Edward Ardizzone's drawings of rather masculine ATS officers and ATS girls flirting (although Ardizzone's depiction of women as flirtatious is by no means restricted to the ATS). A more respectful, admiring view of women in the military can be seen in Anthony Gross's lively watercolours of ATS members being trained in a range of technical areas. Yet where Gross emphasises the novelty of women in technical areas, Schmolle shows them as serious, absorbed and effective.

Another hotly debated issue was women's involvement in combat duties. Women's Auxiliary Air Force (WAAF) Corporal Daphne Pearson, the first female recipient of the Empire Gallantry Medal (later the George Cross), casts an interesting perspective on this. Sitting for a portrait by Dame Laura Knight, Pearson reported in a letter to her mother that Knight was painting her holding a rifle. The final painting includes a respirator instead, but it is not clear when or at whose instigation the portrait was altered.

Ethel Gabain

Sandbag Filling, Islington Borough Council 1941

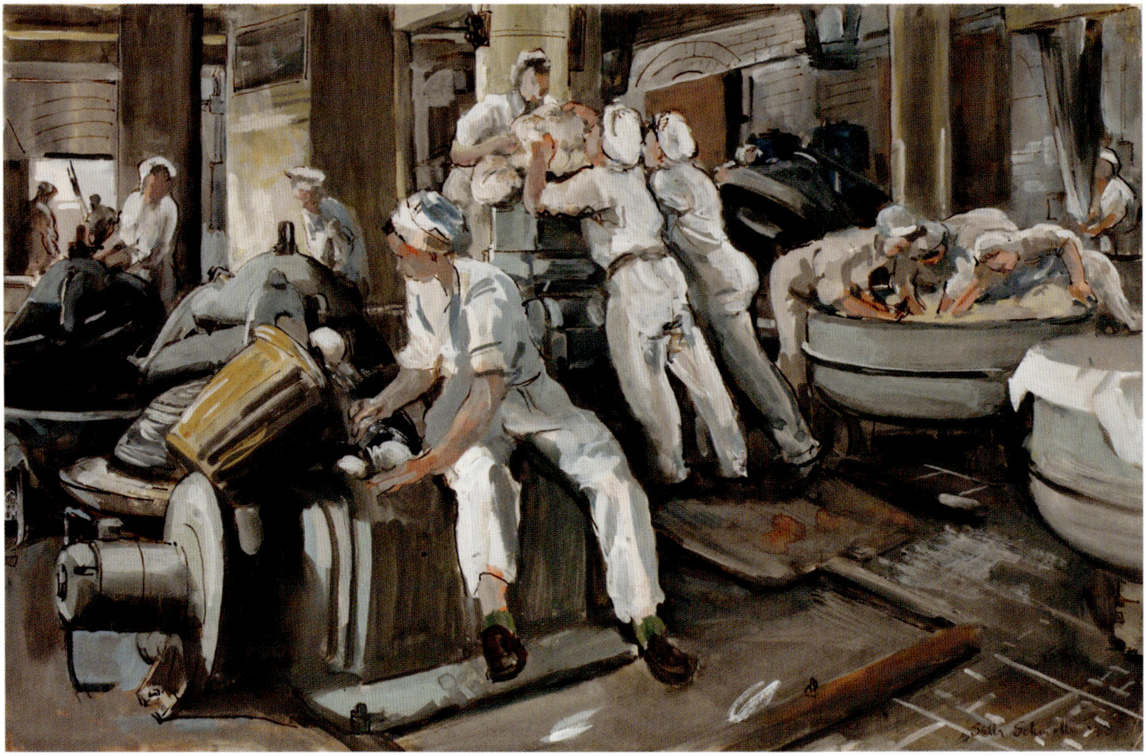

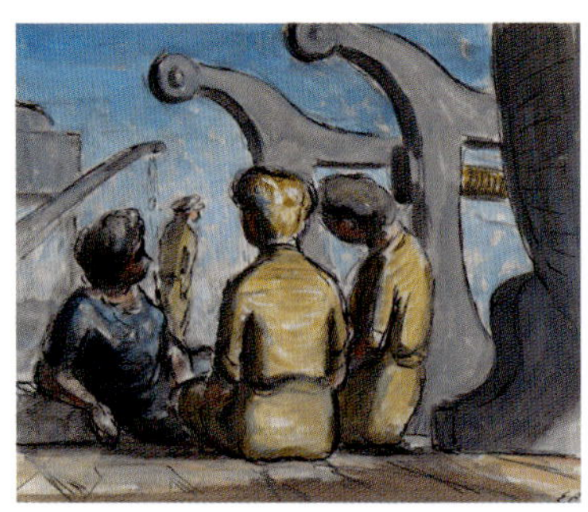

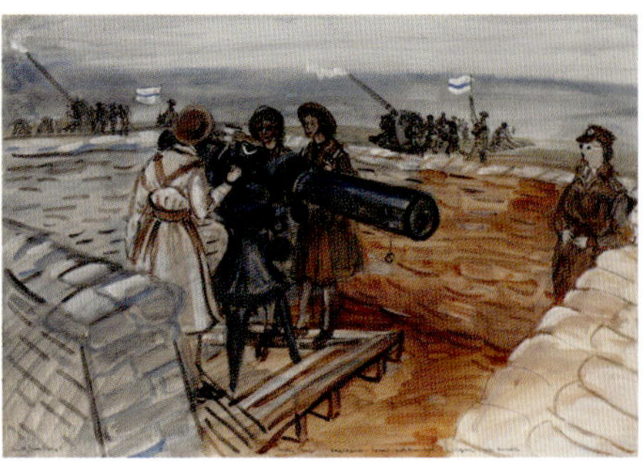

Stella Schmolle

Above: *The Dough Room: Aldershot Command Bakery* 1943

Far left: Edward Ardizzone *ATS on the Boat Deck* 1942

Left: Anthony Gross *An ATS Practice Camp: Height-finding squad with a Kiné Theolodite operator checking results* 1941

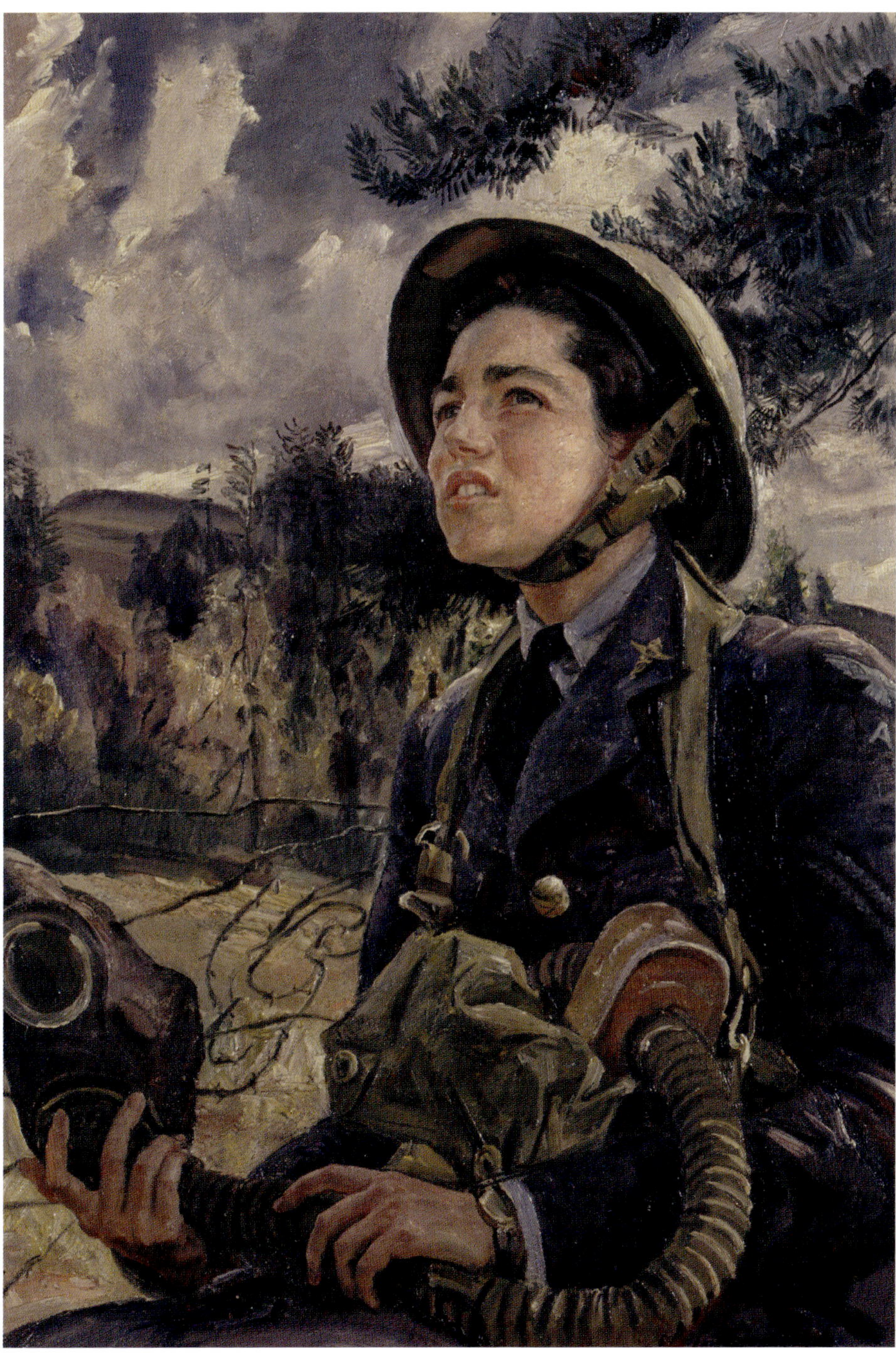

Laura Knight

Left: *Corporal Daphne Pearson* 1940

'I am being painted in a tin helmet and holding a rifle – Air Min. [Air Ministry] will be furious but Dame Laura says my helmet is rather like a bonnet on the back of my head and the rifle makes a good line – WAAFs are "not to carry arms", controversy is still raging and this will upset the apple cart. Dame Laura is adamant and firm.'

Corporal Daphne Pearson GC, the first female recipient of the Empire Gallantry Medal (later the George Cross), writing to her mother in August 1940 about sitting for a portrait by **Laura Knight**.

(Imperial War Museum Documents and Sound Section)

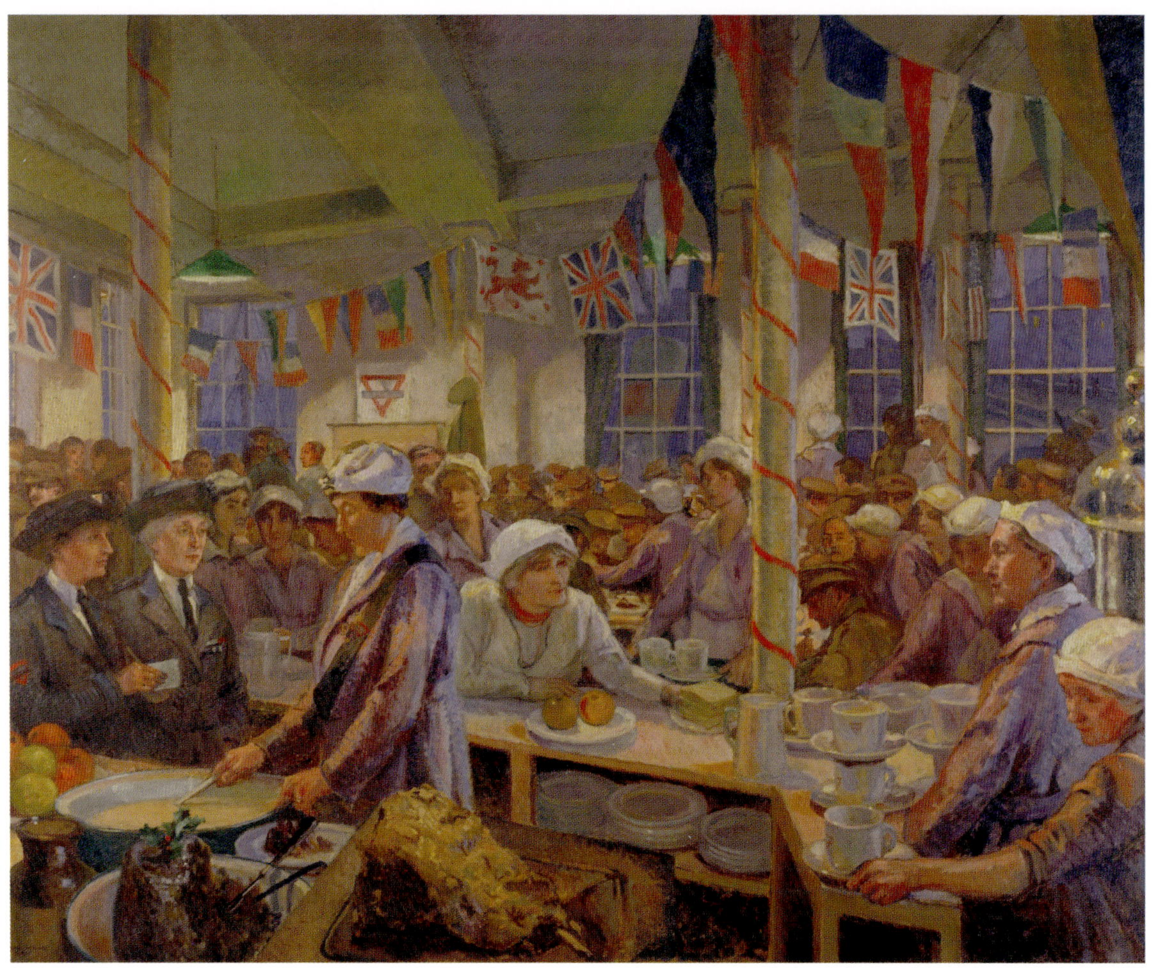

Clare Atwood

Christmas Day in the London Bridge YMCA Canteen 1920

Women as Providers

Through both World Wars women played a vital part in providing food and clothing for troops and civilians. In wartime these traditionally feminine concerns were undertaken and organised on an industrial scale, and supported by women at all stages of production.

Christmas Day in the London Bridge YMCA Canteen was one of the first paintings commissioned by the WWS during the First World War. In this painting Clare Atwood depicts voluntary war workers like the WWS themselves – women with privileged social and political connections who took on leadership roles in women's organisations. Large numbers were recruited into the YMCA's National Women's Auxiliary. Many worked in YMCA canteens providing food and rest for soldiers both behind the lines and at home. Atwood was a well-respected artist, a member of the New English Art Club, and had previously been commissioned through the Canadian War Memorials Fund. Here she captures a warm and festive scene, and creates a successful and atmospheric group portrait.

Evelyn Dunbar worked for the WAAC throughout most of the Second World War, and from 1943 was given several periods as a full-time salaried artist – a unique position for a female artist. Dunbar was also one of the earliest appointments, included in the first wave of artists announced in *The Times* on 25 April 1940.[3] Dunbar was best known as an illustrator and muralist, often working collaboratively with her former teacher and close friend Charles Mahoney. She had studied at the Royal College of Art (RCA) not long after fellow war artists Edward Bawden and Eric Ravilious and, like them, was inspired by English rural life and landscapes. Her commissions cover a wide range of women's experiences, but as a plantswoman and countrywoman she felt particular affinity for the work of the Land Army.

Dunbar's Land Army paintings show the challenges recruits encountered as they learnt new skills and adapted to a new environment. In *Milking Practice with Artificial Udders*, the concentration and patience of the women at their task contrasts with its slight absurdity. Dunbar's paintings are deceptively simple and straightforward, and yet the artist pays extraordinary attention to composition and paint thickness, patterns, light and texture. Her most accomplished painting, *A Land Girl and the Bail Bull*, is one of the masterpieces of the Second World War. She had been encouraged in her career before the war by John Rothenstein, Director of the Tate Gallery, so it was perhaps not surprising that he selected this work as part of the gallery's allocation of war art in 1946.

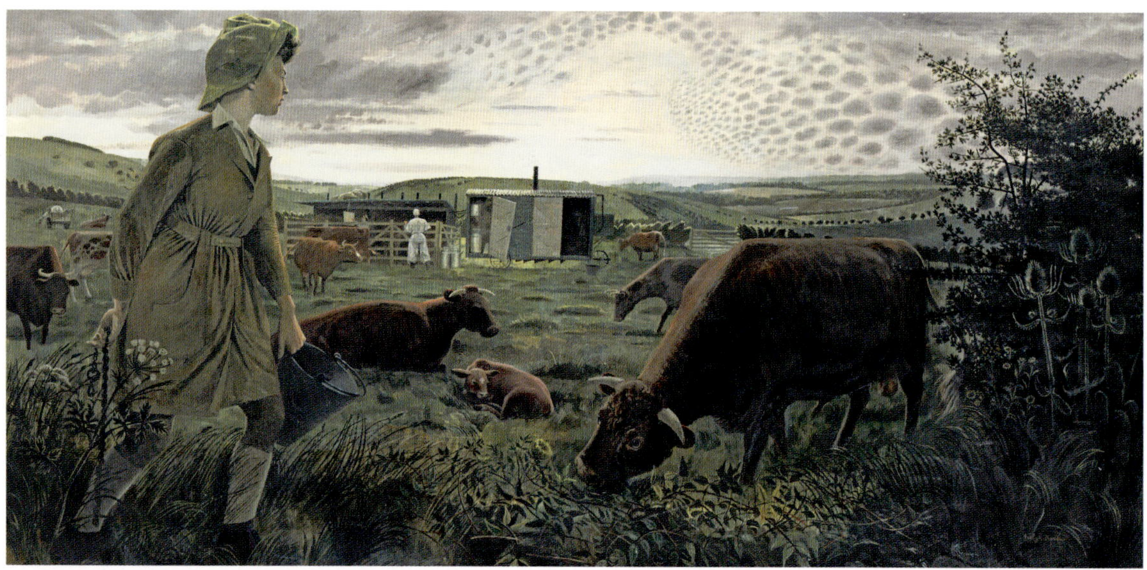

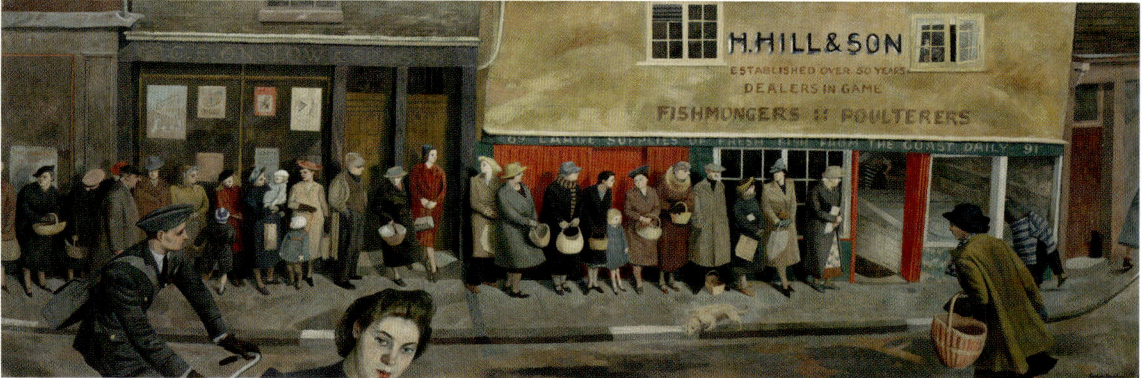

Evelyn Dunbar

Top: *A Land Girl and the Bail Bull* 1945
Bottom: *The Queue at the Fish-shop* 1944

Dunbar's commissions also depict the privations of daily life during rationing. *The Queue at the Fish-shop* is a quirky, individual expression of life in the artist's home town of Rochester, Kent. Her gentle sense of humour is evident in the sign reading 'Large supplies of fresh fish from the coast daily', since normal fishing was restricted both by the Royal Navy's requisitioning of boats and German naval activity. Fish was never rationed because of its perishability, and so was highly sought after despite its scarcity. The painting also incorporates the artist and her family amongst the townsfolk – Dunbar looks out at the viewer from the foreground, while her husband cycles past. Her sister crosses the road briskly with her basket, while her brother stands in the doorway of Onslow and Sons, wearing a cap and with his head cocked to the side.[4]

Clothing manufacture is another theme in Dunbar's works for the WAAC, which often include groups of women working together. In *An Army Tailor and an ATS Tailoress* Dunbar shows male and female tailors working side by side, one woman adopting the tailor's traditional cross-legged working posture. The fabric pools around the figures in elegant spiralling forms. Pegaret Keeling's images of uniform manufacture on the other hand show workers in a more industrialised and mechanised environment. Her work shares some of the wry observational humour of Edward Ardizzone. Although the WAAC did not purchase Keeling's uniform production drawings, they purchased one other small work and assisted her with a permit to draw.

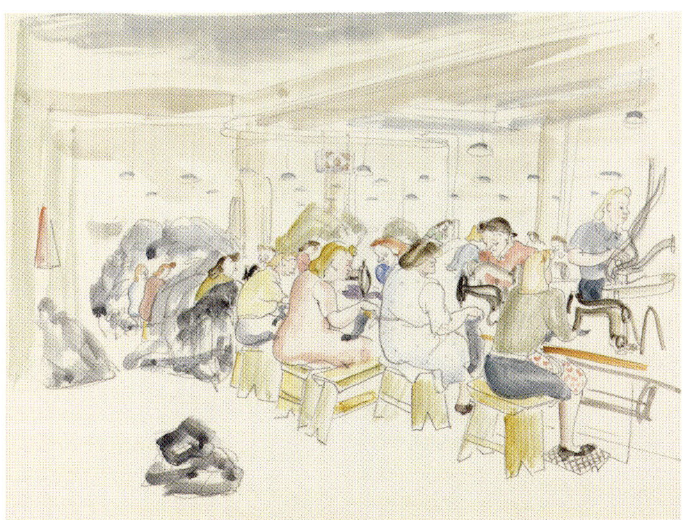

Pegaret Keeling

Right: *Steaming Uniforms*
1943

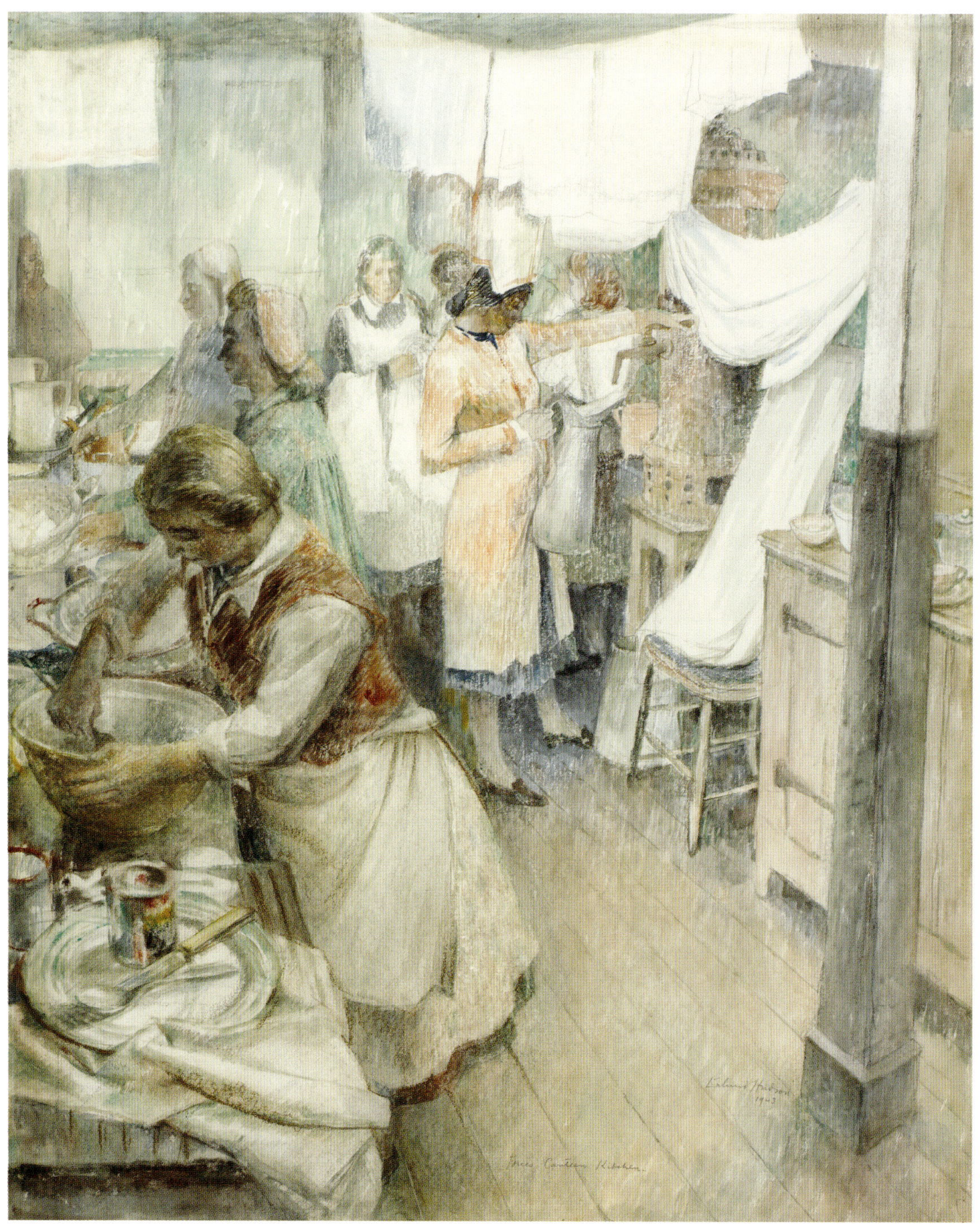

Eleanor (Erlund) Hudson

Left: *Forces Canteen Kitchen* 1943
Below left: *Forces Canteen* 1942

'I think that artists can see in all kinds of circumstances and conditions, design and beautiful compositions whatever the subject.'

Eleanor (Erlund) Hudson, in an interview for the Imperial War Museum Sound Archive.

(Imperial War Museum Documents and Sound Section)

Rozanne Hawksley

Below right: *For Alice Hunter* 2003. From *The Seamstress & the Sea*

Forces Canteen Kitchen was purchased for the WAAC from Eleanor (Erlund) Hudson as an independent submission. Interestingly they did not acquire its counterpart, *Forces Canteen*. This was acquired by the IWM much later, directly from the artist. An image of rest may not have been in the spirit of civilian effort which the WAAC wanted to capture, or this female gaze into a very male space may have aroused a sense of unease – instances of women artists depicting male environments are unusual amongst commissioned works.

Reflecting on women's work in past conflicts, Rozanne Hawksley draws on her own family history. Her grandmother Alice Hunter was an outworker for a Portsmouth naval tailor in the First World War. *For Alice Hunter* is one element of a multi-part installation, *The Seamstress & the Sea*, which meditates on the interaction between seamstress and sailor, from the production of the first collar to the creation of a shroud. *Surgeon's Equipment* takes the theme in a different direction, considering the surgeon's role in suturing the sailor's wounds, and connecting this back to the female seamstress' task. Together the whole forms a subtle and thoughtful evocation of the memory of both sailor and seamstress.

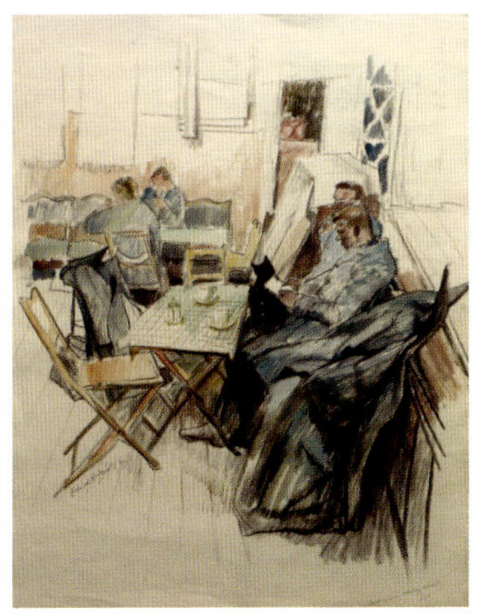

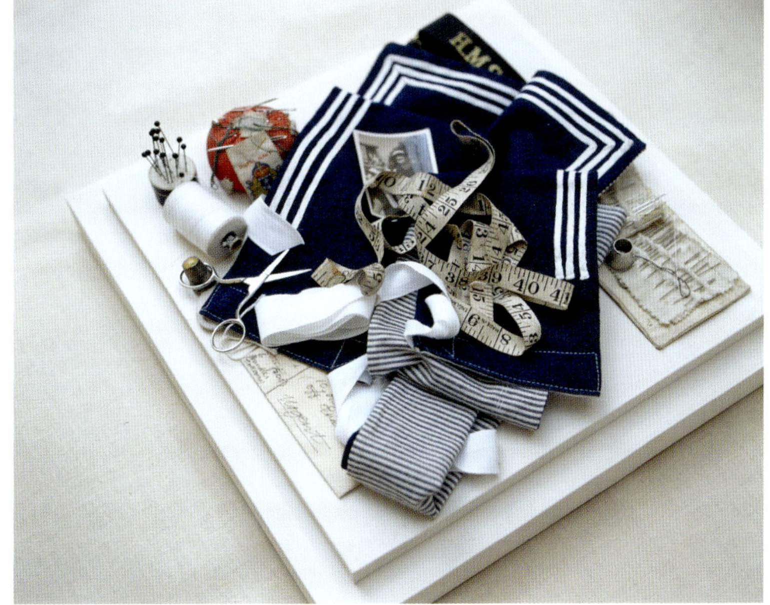

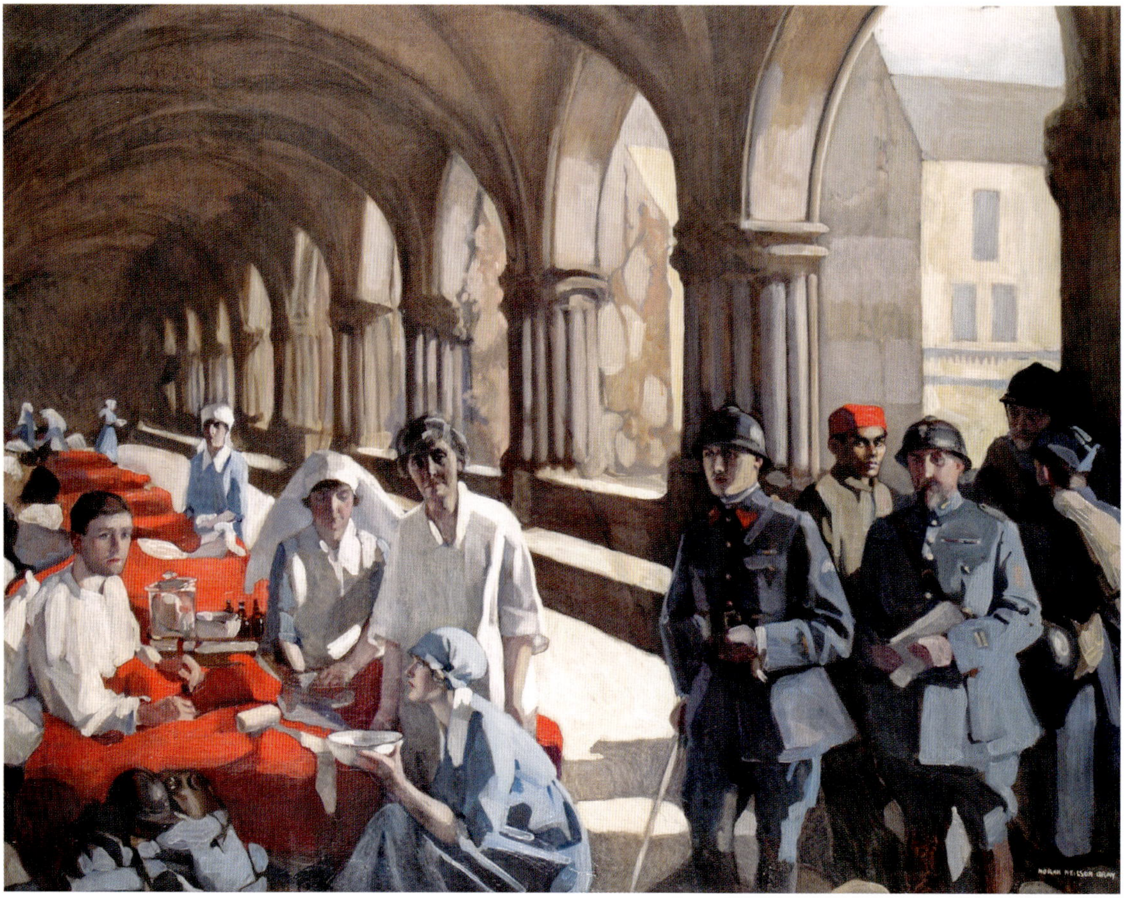

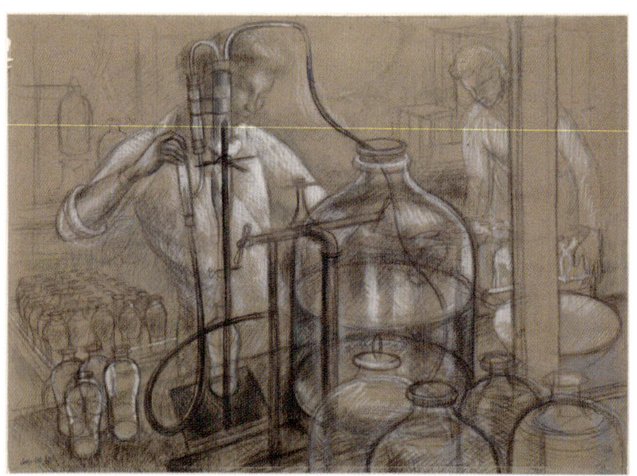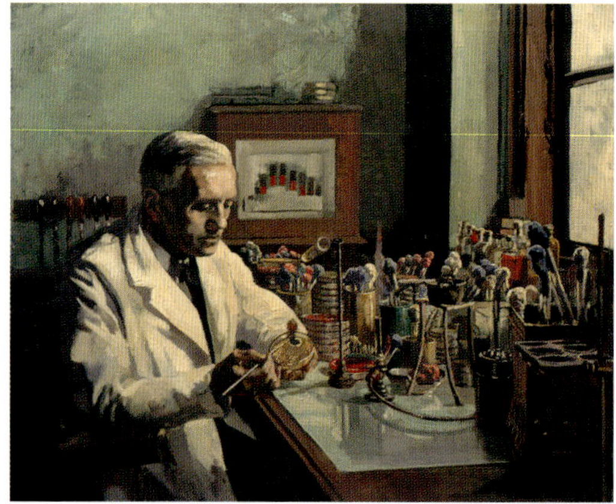

Women and Medicine

The Scottish artist Norah Neilson-Gray nursed for the Scottish Women's Hospitals (SWH) during the First World War. She had already painted *Royaumont in Hôpital Auxiliaire 1918* and offered this painting to the IWM, but the WWS instead pressed her to produce a new work with a greater emphasis on the female doctor. WWS members had personal interests in women's medical work: Lady Norman had helped to run a hospital in France in 1914, and WWS secretary Agnes Conway had been involved in assisting wounded Belgian refugees.

This emphasis on women as dominant participants in medical care was largely absent from the work of male war artists. Their work reflects the broader reality of male doctors carrying out operations and treating wounds, with female nurses and auxiliaries as their subordinates. Paintings of front line casualty clearing stations show only male medical personnel because women were barred from these areas.

The WAAC's coverage of women's work in the Second World War contains more images of nurses than appropriate to the actual proportion of women working in that capacity, and comparatively few of women in other jobs. In all the upheaval of wartime the role of nurse seemed to fit reassuringly with pre-war expectations of women as carers and nurturers.[5] However women's work in the medical services included not only standard nursing care, but also skilled tasks such as blood transfusion. Female artists were keen to show women engaged in technical work they would have been much less likely to do in peacetime. The intricate equipment involved in preparing blood for storage and transfusion attracted the attention of Evelyn Gibbs, fulfilling a WAAC commission. Her charcoal drawings capture the sinuous curves of the tubing and the gleaming glass bottles.

Ethel Gabain chose to focus on innovative medical treatments, particularly the development of penicillin. She painted two oils on this subject – a portrait of its discoverer Alexander Fleming, and *A Child Bomb-Victim Receiving Penicillin Treatment*.[6] Gabain uses bright colour very skilfully, creating harmonious tonalities across her paintings. Another innovation which captured the artist's imagination was a pioneering burns treatment involving continuous irrigation with sodium hypochlorite solution (commonly known by the brand name Milton). Britain's prowess in science and engineering was also a key propaganda message for the WAAC to support. Medical advances in treating burns also interested Anna Zinkeisen – she painted leading plastic surgeon Archibald McIndoe.

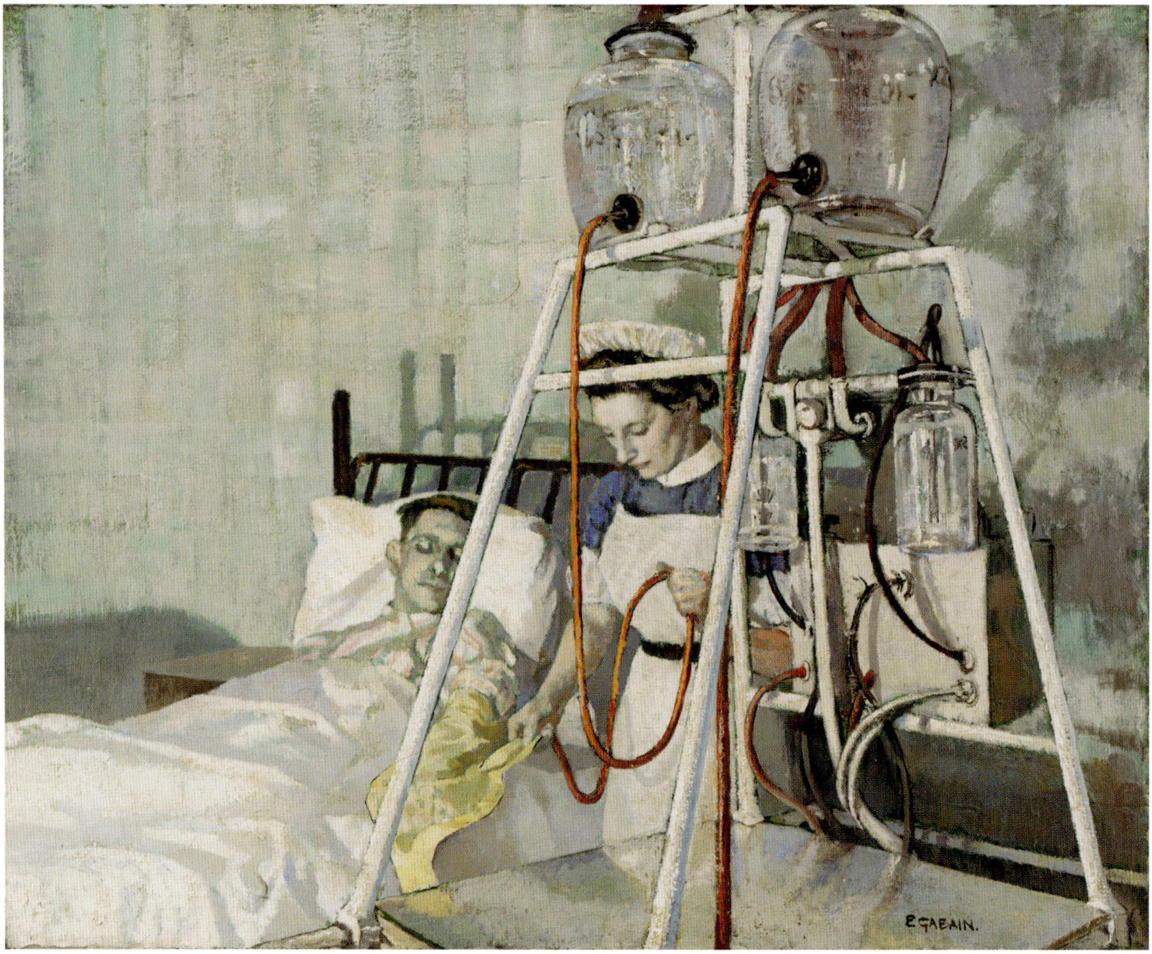

Ethel Gabain

Above: *A Bunnyan-Stannard Irrigation Envelope for the Treatment of Burns being applied by Sister Roberts in Middlesex Hospital* 1943–4

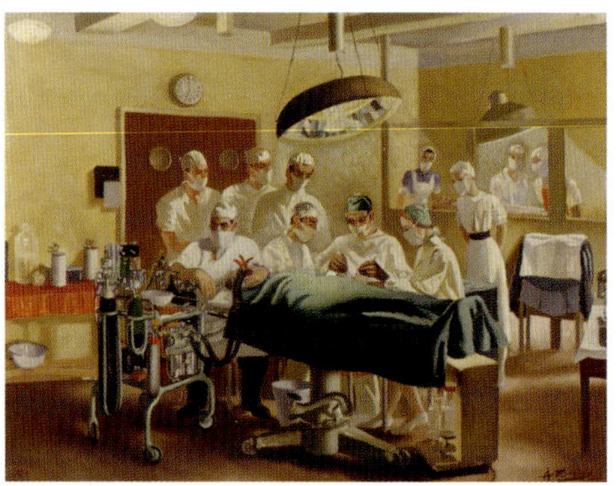

Anna Zinkeisen

Left: *Archibald McIndoe: Consultant in Plastic Surgery to the Royal Air Force, operating at the Queen Victoria Plastic and Jaw Injury Centre, East Grinstead* 1944

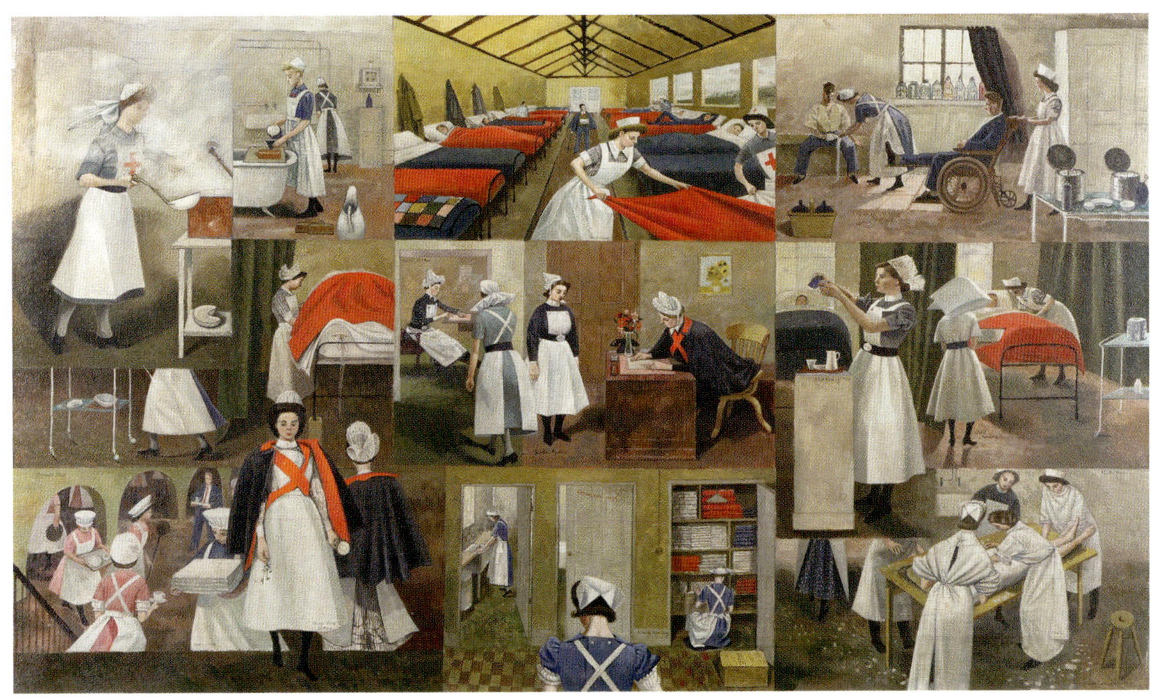

Evelyn Dunbar

Above: *St Thomas's Hospital In Evacuation Quarters* 1942

Zinkeisen worked as a nursing auxiliary, giving her an insider's perspective on medical services. It took great commitment to continue painting while also doing demanding war work.

With her background in book illustration and mural painting, Evelyn Dunbar had a liking for composite designs with a narrative structure, a format she had used for her pre-war painting *An English Calendar*. She used it to effect in two wartime compositions, to describe a female ambulance driver being kitted out in anti-gas clothing, and to convey the multiplicity of tasks involved in running a hospital (*St Thomas' Hospital in Evacuation Quarters*).

'It arose from the vivid impression I received on first going into and going about in a big hospital. My original idea before I went there, was to do a record of the different Nurses in their various uniforms, but their activity transmuted this ... The whole is a scene of everyday hospital tasks, a flat chequered background, with its wreath of crisply white aproned figures moving deftly and swiftly over it.'

Evelyn Dunbar writes to the War Artists Advisory Committee to assist them in preparing an exhibition catalogue entry for the painting, 4 January 1944.

(Imperial War Museum War Artists Archive)

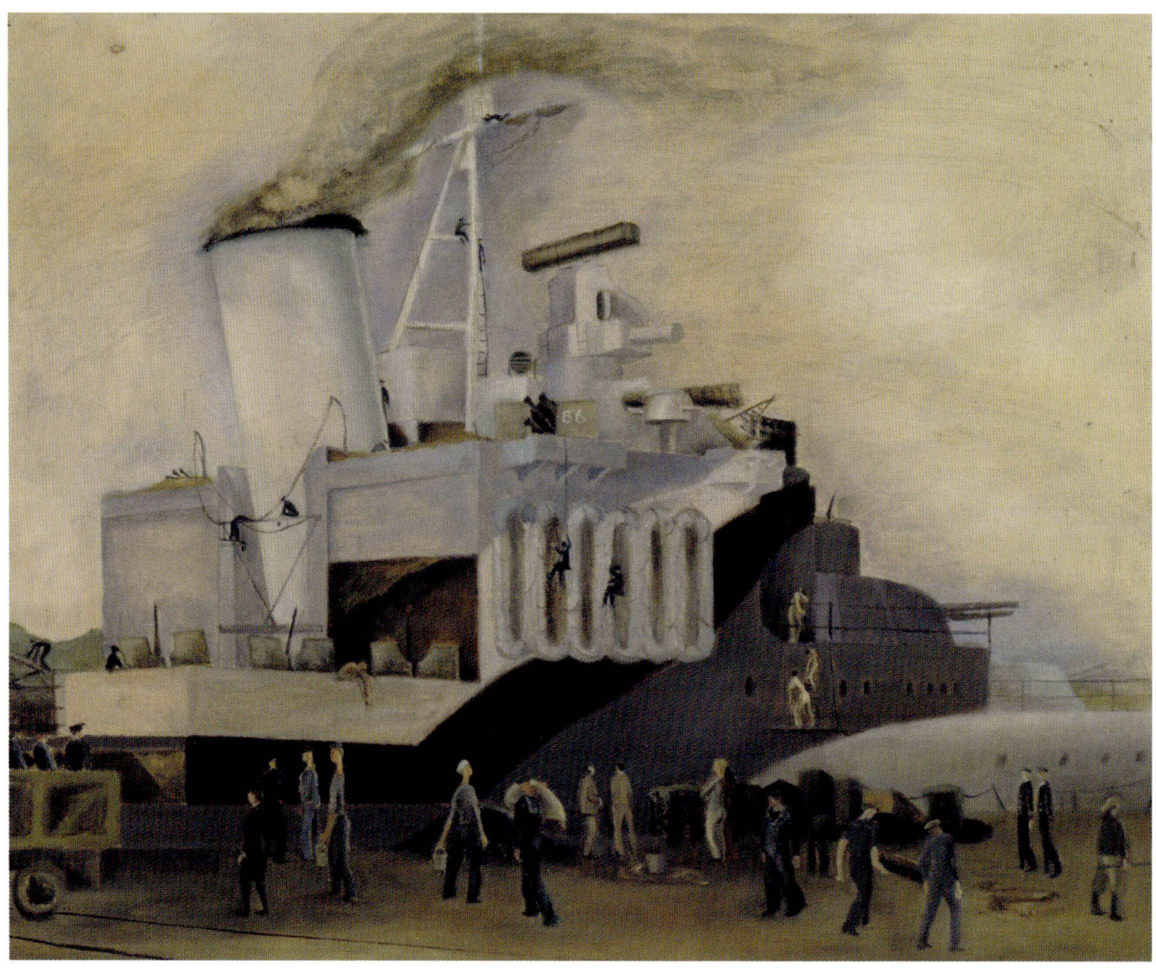

Victorine Foot

Above: *Camouflaging a Cruiser in Dock* 1943

'I really felt I was doing a great job, and one was with
the artists, using paint and colour. I don't think it
could have been a better job really – the atmosphere,
the relationship with other artists.'

In a 1993 interview with the Imperial War Museum Sound Archive,
Victorine Foot describes the artistic milieu at Leamington Spa.

(Imperial War Museum Documents and Sound Section)

During the Second World War private patronage of the arts suffered. Indeed unemployment for artists was recorded at seventy-three per cent in a survey of early 1940.[7] Sir Kenneth Clark, the influential Director of the National Gallery and Chairman of the WAAC, was also instrumental in the Pilgrim Trust's *Recording Britain* project. This project, which ran from 1940–3, sought to record the threatened architectural heritage of the country. It provided a valuable source of employment for artists who were not conscripted due to age, health or gender. One such artist was Phyllis Ginger, who created restrained architectural watercolours for the project.

Other artists were fortunate to find, or to be conscripted into wartime work such as war publicity, camouflage development and cartography which utilised their artistic skills. Conscription applied to women in increasing numbers from late 1941, and disrupted the progress of many young artists through art school. For example Victorine Foot interrupted her art studies to work in the Civilian Camouflage Directorate at Leamington Spa from 1940–4. Foot was able to carry on her own work by drawing and painting her colleagues in the unit, and successfully submitted a painting for purchase by the WAAC. Her informal sketches, which she later donated to the IWM, capture some of the personalities involved, and describe techniques used to test camouflage designs.

Victorine Foot

Below left: *Directorate of Camouflage (Naval Section) at work, Leamington Spa, 1941* 1941

Below right: *Officers of the Directorate of Camouflage (Naval Section) at work in the Art Gallery, Leamington Spa, 1941* 1941

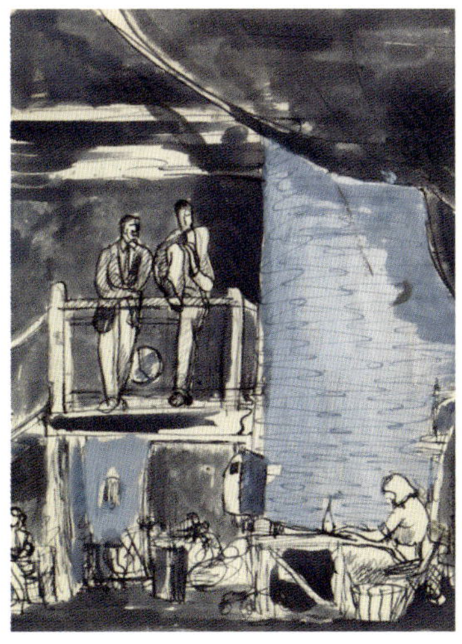

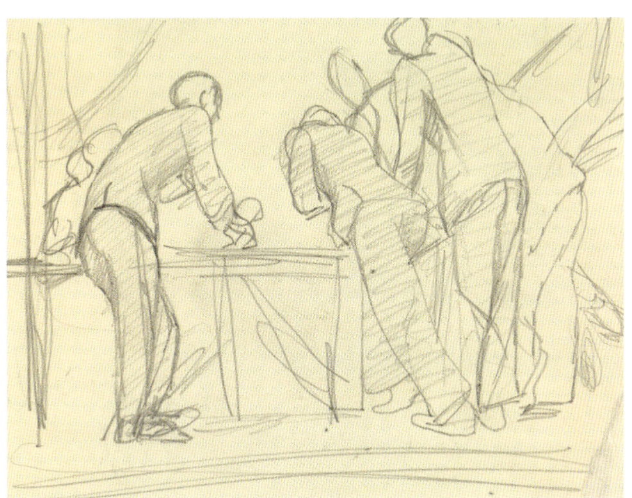

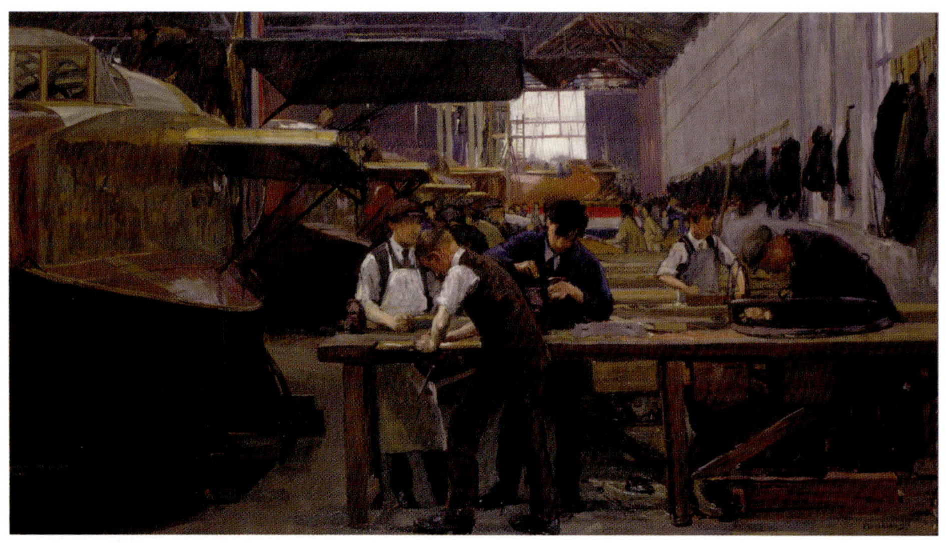

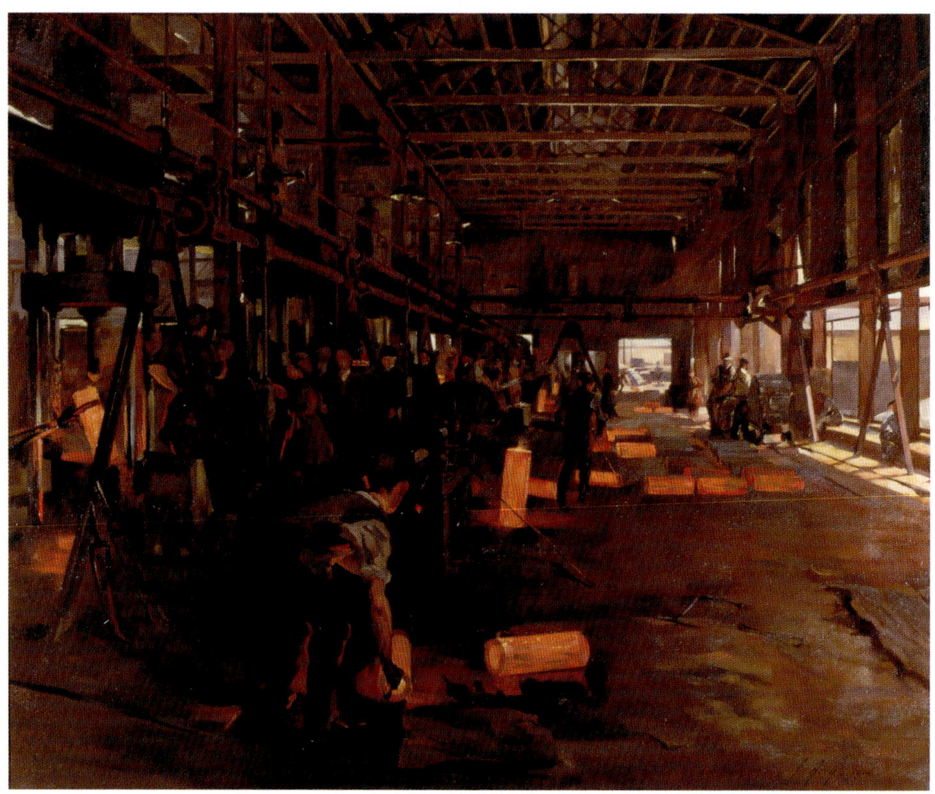

Enormous numbers of women in both World Wars worked in factories producing weapons, often in low-skilled and repetitive jobs. Nearly a million women worked in the munitions industry during the First World War, and many of the images commissioned from women artists show female weapons workers and their surroundings.[8] Women were already working in factories before the war, but had been concentrated in particular industries and earned low wages. The introduction of male conscription in 1916 prompted an expansion of opportunities for women entering previously male roles.

There was strong opposition from male workers' unions to women taking up skilled work or achieving equal pay. The agreed solution was 'dilution', where complex tasks were broken down into simpler stages for women workers. Women, however, continued to press for equal pay in substituting for male workers – many were struggling on meagre separation allowances with husbands, fathers and sons away.

Weapons manufacture was a relatively well-paid role for women, offering real independence. In Flora Lion's *Women's Canteen at Phoenix Works, Bradford, 1918*, women weapons workers are seen as a sisterhood of bold, handsome young women (see inside front cover). Canteens were a popular wartime welfare innovation, aimed at maximising production. For many women it was their first opportunity to enjoy a good regular meal.[9] This was a rare MOI commission for a woman artist, and the Ministry arranged Lion's access to the factories. Government spending was fiercely cut back after the war, and funds were tight, nevertheless it is symptomatic of the treatment of women artists that the painting was not purchased by the IWM (which oversaw the winding up of the MOI war art scheme after the MOI was abolished in 1918). Two of Lion's paintings were eventually donated to the IWM in the late 1920s, with a supportive patron paying the artist for one of them.

Anna Airy also experienced difficulty with her MOI commission – her painting was rejected. A separate commission from the IWM's Munitions Committee resulted in four paintings. In *A Shell Forge at a National Projectile Factory, Hackney Marshes, London* Airy captures the dramatic colours of the hot steel, the huge open space of the factory floor, and the complex light from furnaces and sunlight. Lion's *Building Flying-boats* is a cooler, quieter painting. The male workers are shown gathered at their work bench, giving a very different impression from the female workers in Lion's canteen

Flora Lion

Top left: *Building Flying Boats* 1918

Anna Airy

Left: *A Shell Forge at a National Projectile Factory, Hackney Marshes, London* 1918

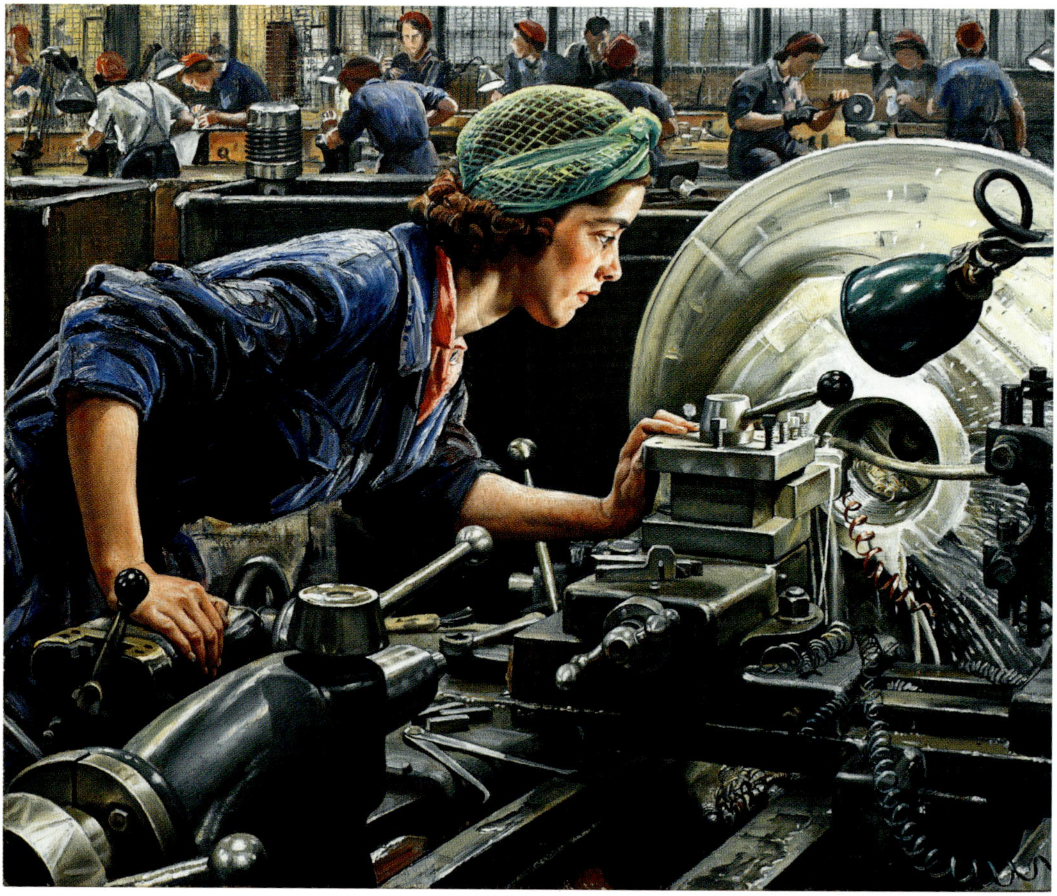

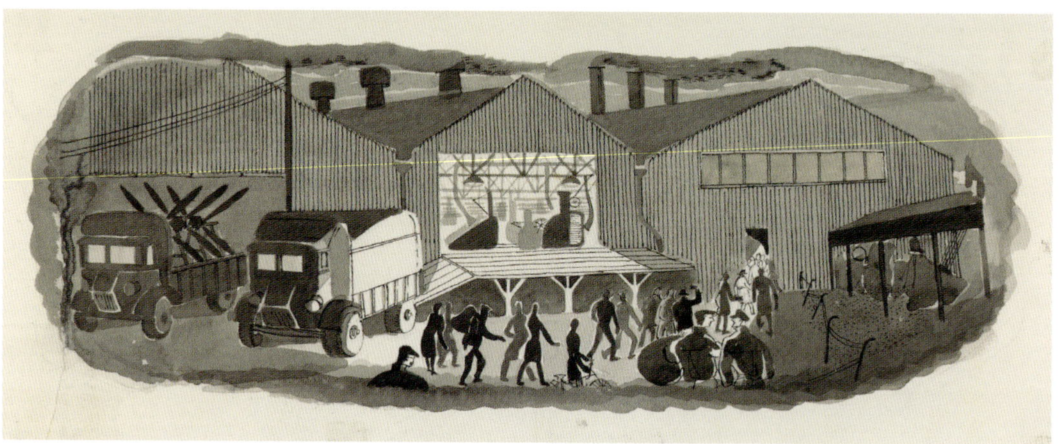

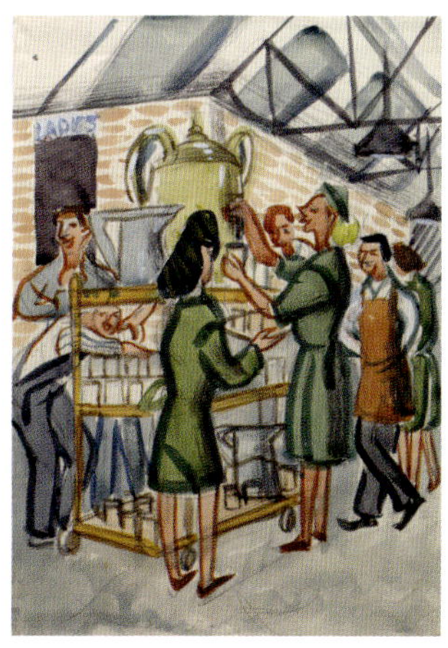

painting. These are likely to have been skilled cabinet makers, conscious of their higher status.

Airy and Lion were unusual amongst the official women war artists of the First World War in entering and recording male workplaces. In Lion's case this may have been due to the genesis of her commissions in the MOI scheme, and for Airy was the result of an unusual commission for a woman from the IWM's Munitions Committee. Both artists enjoyed successful careers, and had a high reputation at the time, having exhibited regularly in the Royal Academy. They have since suffered a degree of neglect, along with many male artists of their generation, their quieter skill obscured by the triumphant arrival of Modernism.

During the Second World War women were again drawn into industrial production in very large numbers, but men continued to occupy the most highly skilled factory jobs. Despite the introduction of conscription for young single women in December 1941, the Ministry of Supply (MOS) had problems with the recruitment and retention of women in industry. Women were leaving in part due to problems with childcare, but were also demotivated by resistance to using them in skilled roles.[10]

The MOS recommended Ruby Loftus, 'an outstanding factory worker', to the WAAC as a subject. In late 1942 Laura Knight was commissioned to paint her, and as a result Loftus quickly became something of a celebrity. Loftus worked at the Royal Ordnance Factory in Newport. At twenty-one, and with no previous industrial experience, she had mastered the complex skill of making a breech ring for the Bofors gun, the most highly skilled job in the factory. The gun could be highly dangerous if this task was not carried out correctly, and it was usually undertaken by a worker of eight or nine years' experience.[11]

The choice of Knight for the commission was apt: already a Dame, and the first woman to be elected a Royal Academician in over 150 years, she too was succeeding in a traditionally male environment. It also underlines, however, the tendency for successful women to be singled out as exceptional individuals, with the underlying implication that few women were capable of such success. Knight excels in presenting Loftus as an exceptional and glamorous role model, but the painting does not reflect the gritty reality of women's war work.[12]

As a young artist, Margaret Abbess's conscription into war work delayed her entry to the Royal College of Art – she was sent to work in a factory making springs, a component for Spitfires. Despite not having a permit, Abbess made a series of drawings documenting the factory where she worked which provide an unusual, unofficial insight. In official art from the Second World War men and women are rarely shown working together, and there are few images of rest breaks. In contrast Abbess gives us scenes of male and female workers socialising over the tea urn and at the factory gates. She also draws the cityscapes of her journey to and from work, and the architecture of the factory interior. The factory work was dull and undemanding, and Abbess occupied herself with making brief surreptitious sketches and committing scenes to her visual memory to be set down on paper later.

Like Airy and Lion before her, during the Second World War Frances Macdonald was commissioned to portray the male workplace. A recent graduate from the Royal College of Art, she undertook several specific commissions for the WAAC, and also worked for the *Recording Britain* project. In *43 Group Air Frame Repair Service, Lincoln: Putting Air-Screws in Position by Means of Overhead Cranes*, the artist portrays men working in a vast industrial space in a cool, subtle palette. Known for her work as a landscape painter, Macdonald was attracted to large-scale, industrial scenes. One of her most successful wartime paintings, *Building the Mulberry Harbour, London Docks*, is a wide panorama of the docks with the vast floating harbour components under construction, the skyline punctuated by cranes. This painting, like Dunbar's *Land Girl*, was requested for the Tate Gallery at the distribution of works from the WAAC in 1946, giving an indication of its estimation at that time.

Frances Macdonald

Below: *Building the Mulberry Harbour, London Docks 1944* 1944

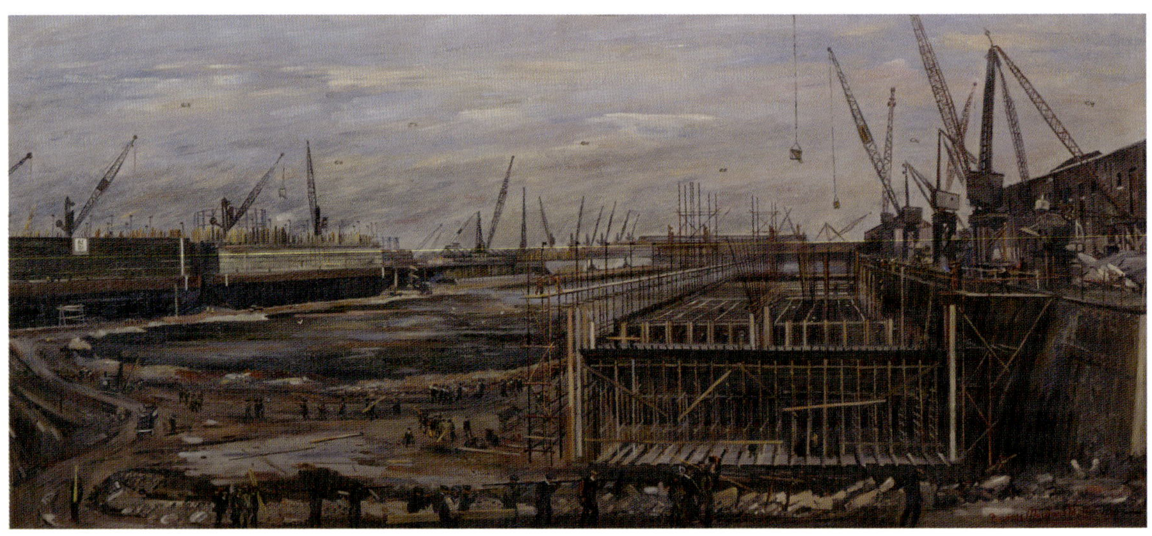

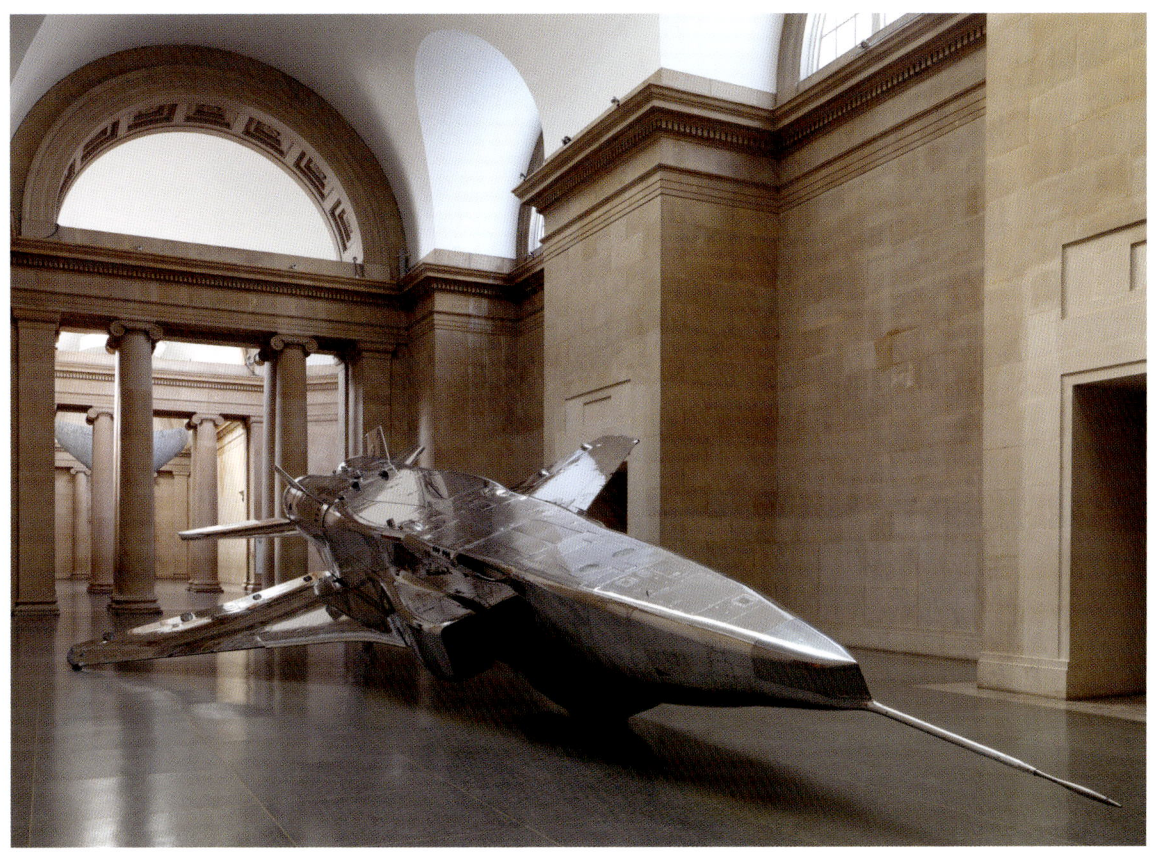

Fiona Banner

Fetishising military hardware, or transgressively reinterpreting it, is an approach taken by a number of female contemporary artists. Fiona Banner has explored these ideas over a long period. She has collected media images of fighter planes, drawn them, and used planes as a canvas for text works in which she describes the female nude. Most recently she has displayed complete planes, in *Harrier and Jaguar* at Tate Britain. The two fighter planes are subtly transformed by the artist: the Jaguar stripped and polished; the Harrier made more intensely bird-like with painted feathers. They hold within them tensions of meaning – are they natural or unnatural, beautiful or terrible, attractive or repulsive? Presented like dead game, or like trophies, they are transformed into objects of worship, like the products of contemporary art. And yet their purpose as killing machines makes this transformation morally unsettling.

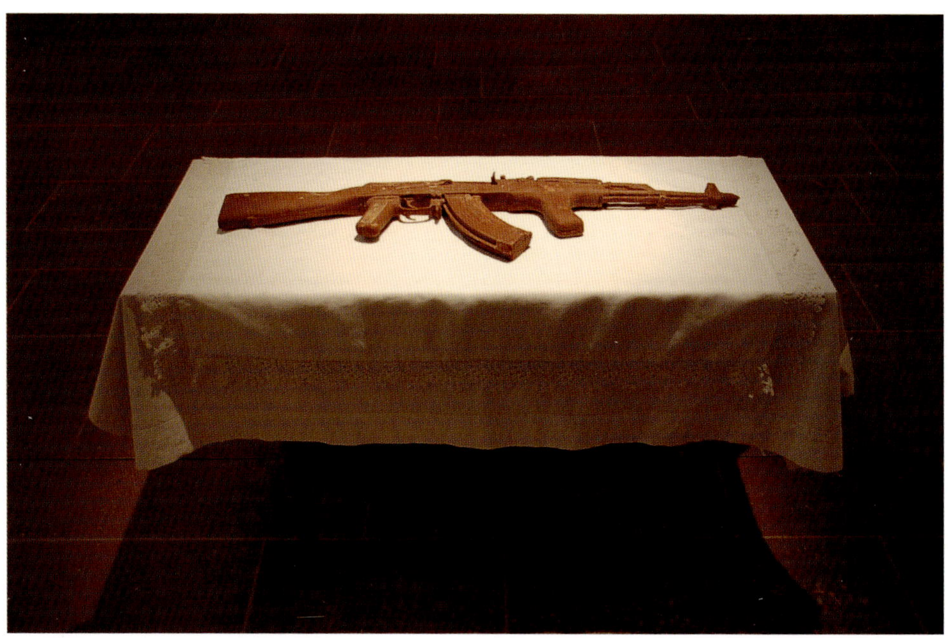

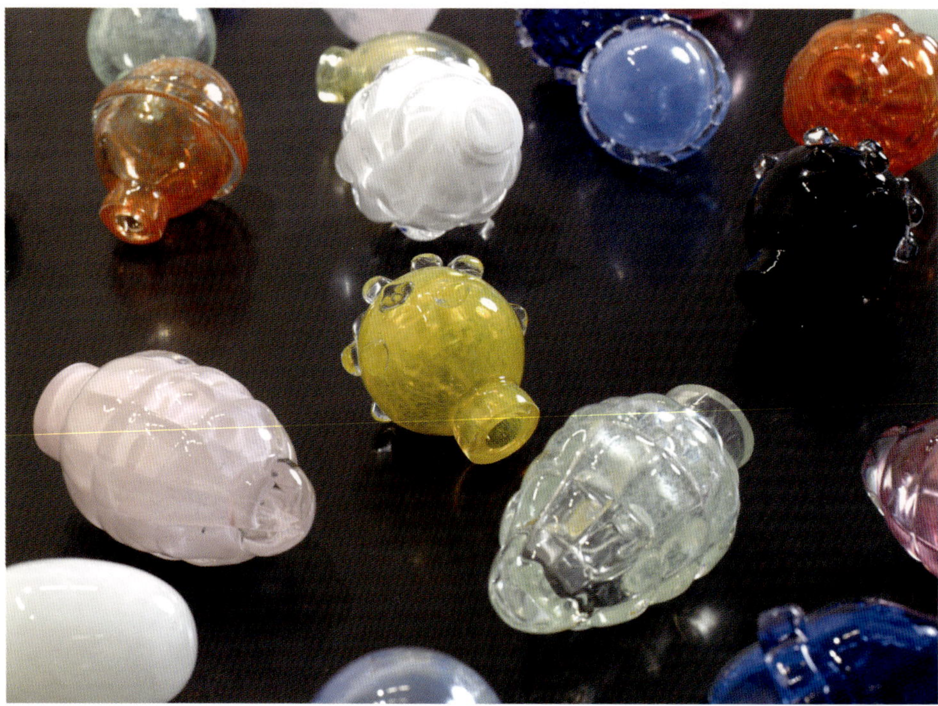

Mona Hatoum has also explored the potential of objects to cause harm, taking seemingly benign objects and transforming them into something lethal or painful. She presents potential violence and allows the viewer to realise it in their own imagination. In *Nature morte aux grenades* 2006–7 Hatoum inverts this, taking hand grenades and rendering them in jewel-like coloured glass, giving them a terrible beauty. Rita Duffy also presents us with a transformed weapon in her work *Dessert*. This chocolate gun is cast from an AK-47 decommissioned through the Northern Ireland peace process. The piece embodies the attraction of violence, the temptation of the empowerment which comes from joining paramilitary organisations. And yet it also implies that violence is ultimately ineffectual since the gun is neutered: only made of chocolate, it cannot be used.

'When I started making these works I was criticized for not showing the "spectacle of horror", but expecting the viewer to imagine for themselves the impending disaster. I personally felt that this was precisely the strength of the work and a sign of maturity in the way the work conjures up certain images in the viewer's mind. That these things are implied through the visual poetry of the work rather than didactically stated is much more satisfying for me.'

Mona Hatoum in conversation with Janine Antoni,
first published in *BOMB Magazine*, No. 63, Spring 1998.

[1] Arthur Marwick, *Women at War 1914–1918*, London 1977, p.166.

[2] Lucy Noakes, *Women in the British Army: War and the Gentle Sex, 1907–48*, London 2006, pp.61–81 and pp.103–32.

[3] Gill Clarke, *Evelyn Dunbar – War and Country*, Bristol 2006, p.83.

[4] Ibid. p.129.

[5] Brian Foss, *War Paint: Art, War, State and Identity in Britain, 1939–1945*, London 2007, pp.83–87.

[6] At the time of writing the portrait is on long loan from the Imperial War Museum to the National Portrait Gallery, London.

[7] Katy Deepwell, *Women Artists Between The Wars, – 'A fair field and no favour'*, Manchester 2010, p.80.

[8] Marwick, *Women at War*, p.166.

[9] Deborah Thom, 'Women and Work In Wartime Britain', *Women, Work and Society 1914–1918*, Cengage resource based on the Women's Work Collection at the Imperial War Museum. <http://www.tlemea.com/thom.asp> accessed 12 Nov.2010.

[10] Foss, *War Paint*, pp.109–11.

[11] Some have since questioned her achievement, implying that she was merely placed at the machine or was undertaking a slightly less complex procedure, but WAAC records provide no evidence for this.

[12] Foss, *War Paint*, pp.111–15.

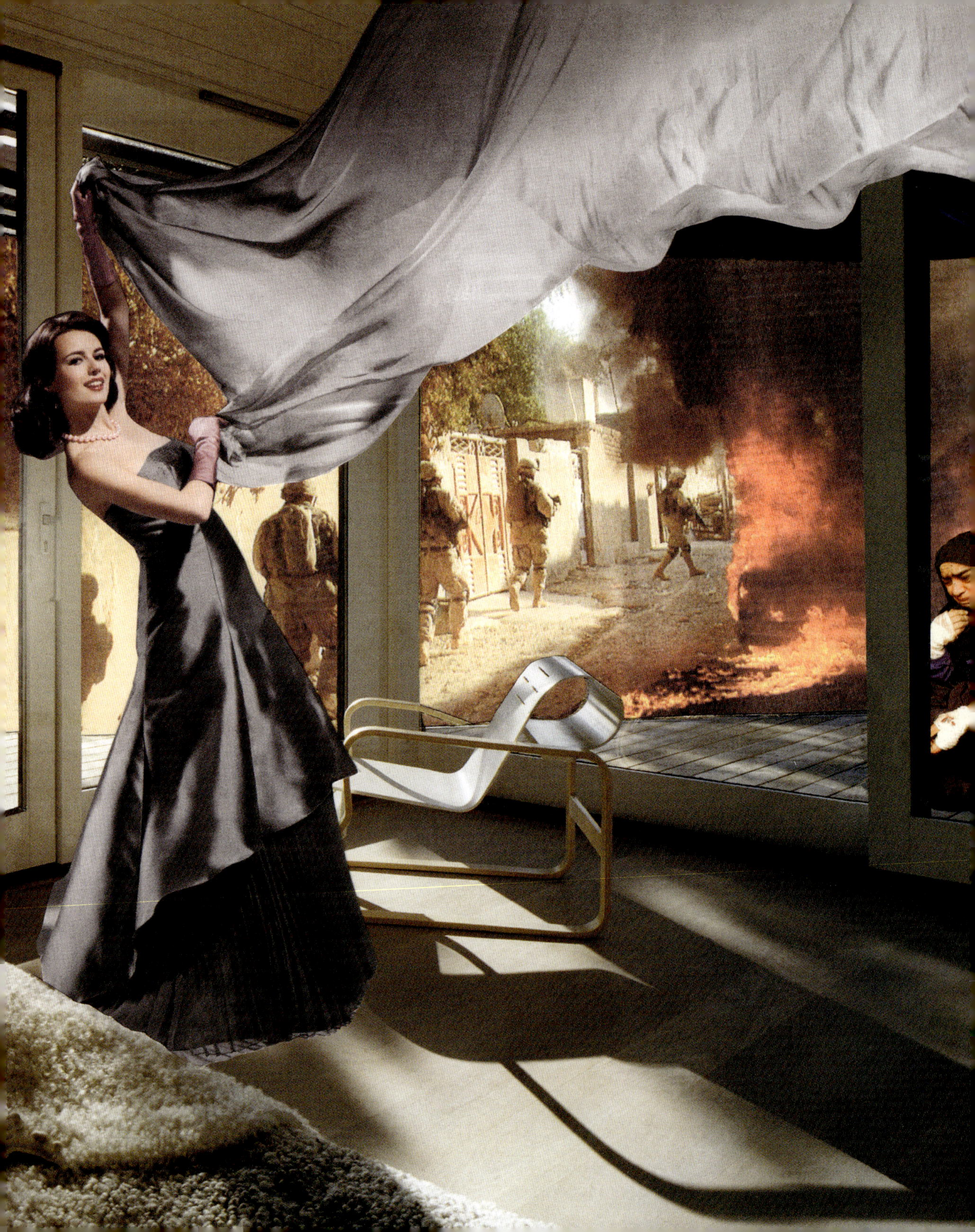

The Costs of War

Women artists have not been afraid to confront some of the most difficult and disturbing consequences of war for individuals and communities: homelessness, exile, occupation, suffering, death and atrocity. Only very rarely, however, has their engagement with these subjects been commissioned or supported by government patronage. This reflects the fact that the direct depiction of civilian suffering on the home front has rarely been officially supported for fear of damaging morale. Although art showing enemy atrocities, real or alleged, was not discouraged, constraints on female access to the theatre of war have made women artists less likely to witness these directly.

Conflicting social attitudes shape responses to female artists addressing horror. Often such artists are identified as exceptional rather than seen as the norm for their gender, or there is an assumption that female artists will excel in empathy. Critics and commentators often seek to identify feminine aspects of female artists' work, which can sometimes obscure its other qualities.

Witnesses of Death and Destruction

The British government war artists scheme of the First World War avoided the hysterical images of alleged German war crimes which appeared in war publicity and popular journalism of the time. It also discouraged and censored images of dead British soldiers.[1] During the Second World War more images of human suffering were commissioned or acquired by the War Artists Advisory Committee (WAAC), but these largely focussed on the inhumanity of the enemy abroad rather than anything closer to home.

On 15 April 1945 British soldiers entered Bergen-Belsen concentration camp to find a scene of absolute horror. From late 1944 thousands of Jewish survivors of death marches from further east had been crammed into a camp originally built for far fewer inmates. Ten thousand corpses lay unburied, and around 60,000 starving and sick people were packed into the camp's barracks without food or water. Doris Zinkeisen, commissioned by the British Red Cross to record their activities in Europe, was one of the artists who arrived soon afterwards. Some of her paintings were later acquired by the WAAC.

Human Laundry is arguably the most powerful work to result from this experience. Zinkeisen finds an effective motif in the contrast between the well fed, rounded bodies of the German carers and the

Martha Rosler

The Gray Drape 2008
Courtesy the artist and Galerie Christian Nagel

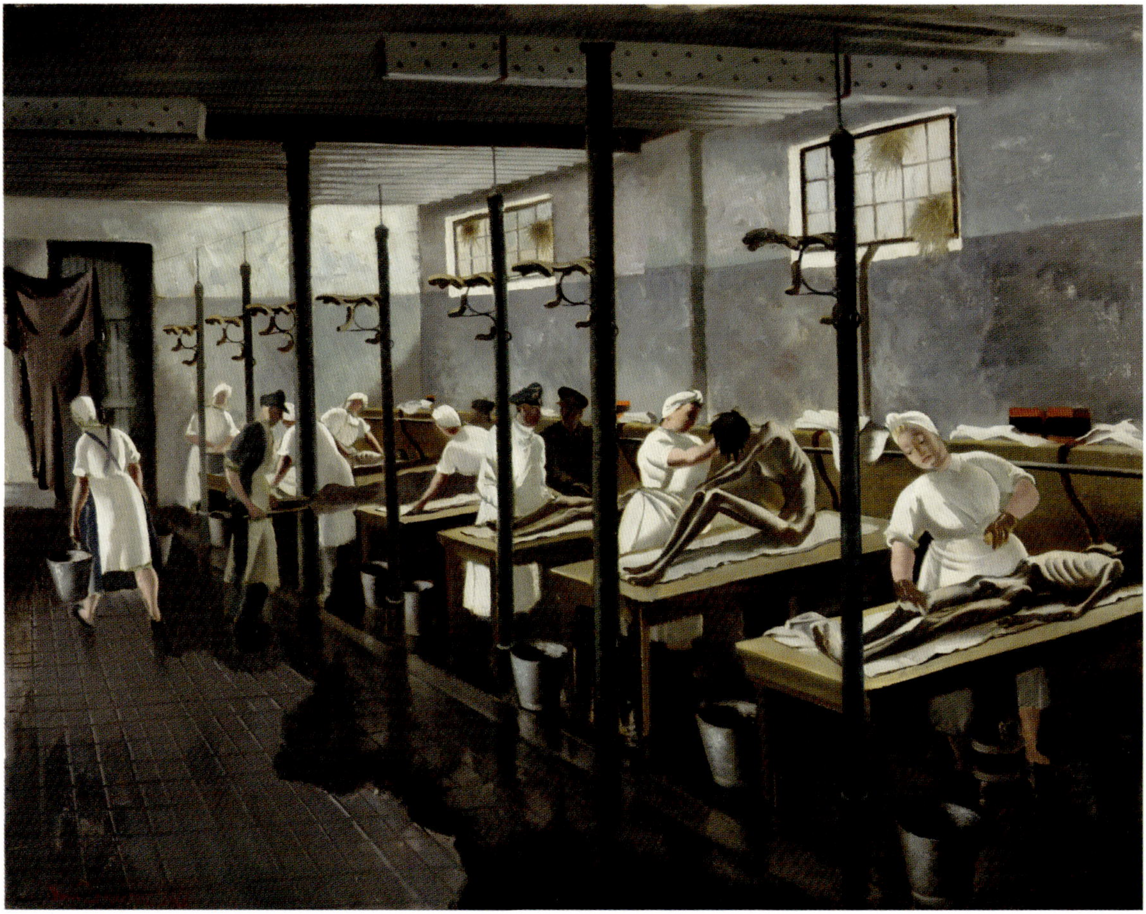

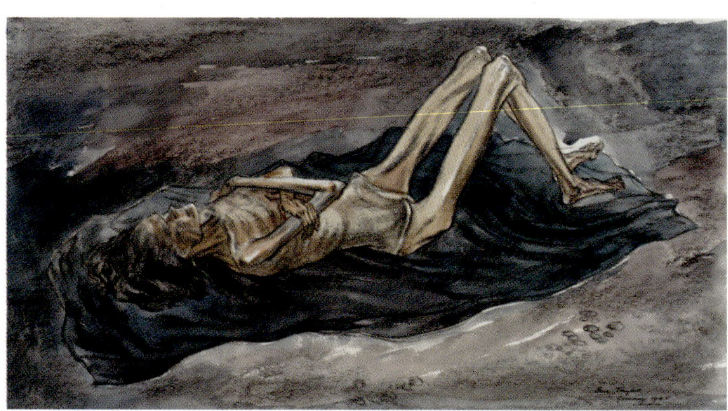

Left: Eric Taylor
Dying from Starvation and
Torture at Belsen Concentration
Camp, 1945 1945

Doris Zinkeisen

'The shock of Belsen was never to be forgotten … The stable was used to wash any living creature down before sending them into hospital to be treated. Each stall had a table on which to lay the patient – the German prisoners did the washing. The church was used as a hospital for those that were alive.'

Doris Zinkeisen remembers her experience in an autobiographical text written for the Imperial War Museum in 1981.

(Imperial War Museum War Artists Archive)

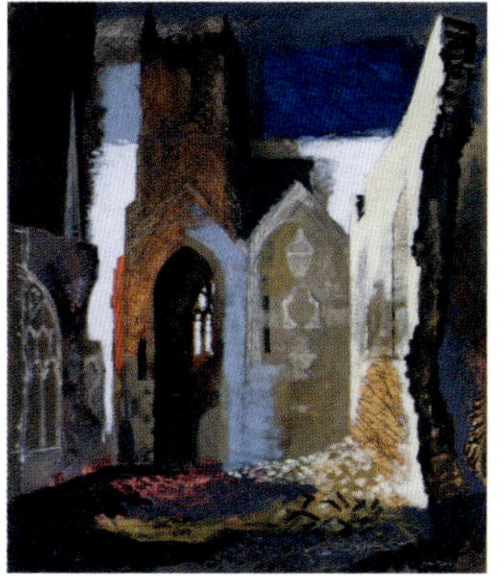

Left: John Piper
St Mary le Port, Bristol 1940

emaciated bodies of their patients. This angry response makes such a strong impact that it may even have led to some misinterpretation. Zinkeisen's own later account refers to the German medical personnel as 'prisoners', implying that they were former concentration camp staff now being detained by the British military. They were actually nurses and doctors from a nearby German military hospital who had been pressed into service.[2] It is the very orderliness, and almost industrial scale of this washing process which serves to underline the extraordinary condition of the patients. This contrast is perhaps lost in the more chaotic scenes of camp conditions outside produced both by Zinkeisen and Leslie Cole. Eric Taylor's large scale watercolour drawings depict individuals in extreme suffering, indeed on the verge of death. This urge as an eye-witness to create a dispassionate record was not gender-specific – a similar attitude is apparent in the work of women photographers such as Lee Miller and Margaret Bourke-White.[3]

German bombing raids caused mass casualties in many British towns and cities, but this subject was addressed quite differently. Images of dead and injured civilians were not commissioned by the WAAC, but on the other hand, there was a boundless appetite for bomb-damaged cityscapes, particularly the apocalyptic architectural ruins painted by John Piper and Graham Sutherland. Far from depressing morale, such scenes may have been thought to celebrate and encourage resilience, but in any case bombed streets and buildings were an everyday sight for many city dwellers. The civilians sheltering in the tunnels of the London Underground were rendered suitably anonymous and sculptural in Henry Moore's work, and in Edward Ardizzone's drawings they appear as jolly, comic types. Female artists' responses to the Blitz might be expected to show some contrasts with such male artists, but on closer investigation the strongest differences can be seen between artists officially commissioned and those working independently. Women artists can be seen working across a full range of artistic styles and responses alongside their male colleagues, albeit with less official support.

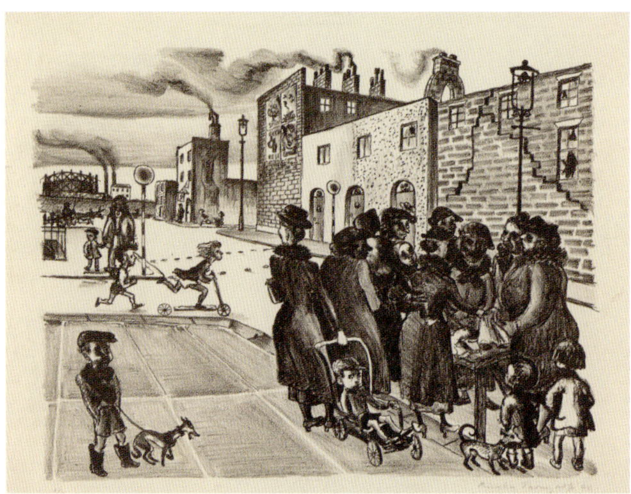

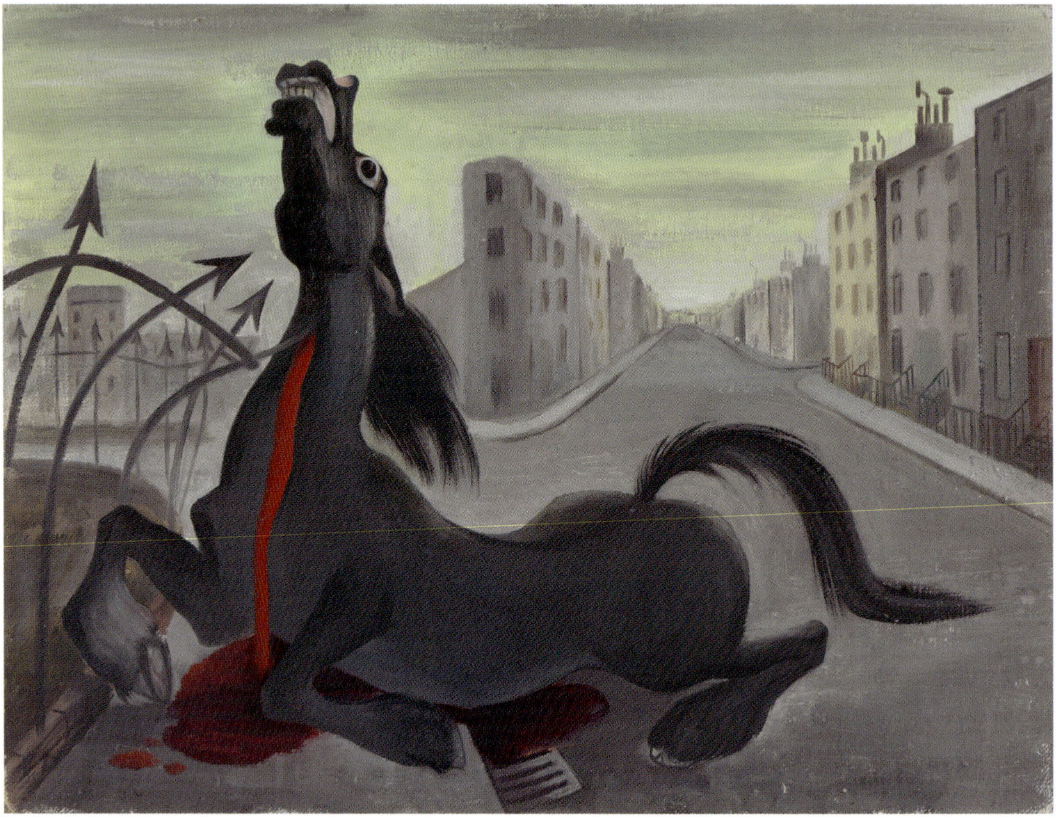

Priscilla Thornycroft's drawings and paintings of life during the Blitz were created independently of the WAAC, and were neither commissioned nor purchased by them. Drawing or taking photographs of sensitive subjects in many public places was tightly controlled by a system of permits, but although Thornycroft did not have one she seems to have escaped detection. Thornycroft's focus on ordinary Londoners in her own Camden Town locality reflects her communist views. She portrays people in a quirky, slightly dark tone, very different to Ardizzone's jolly images or Moore's statuesque shelterers. The artist reveals those affected by the nightly destruction as real individuals, not ennobled and mythologised, nor humorously long-suffering. Her striking painting *Runaway Horse in an Air Raid Alarm* – of a horse so terrified by the siren that it had bolted and impaled itself on railings – seems almost surreal in its nightmare quality, but was based on an incident the artist witnessed and which had stayed vividly in her mind.

Delicate watercolours of bomb-damaged buildings by **Phyllis Ginger** were less controversial, and the WAAC purchased one, while others were acquired by the Pilgrim Trust's *Recording Britain* project. This project was specifically aimed at supporting artists during wartime, when private and industrial work was scarce, as well as recording Britain's endangered architectural heritage. Several artists, such as John Piper, were commissioned by both bodies. Like several artists, male and female, who had come through the lean times of the 1930s, Ginger was adept at applying her artistic skills to practical ends, such as the plate designs she produced for Wedgwood depicting barrage balloons over London.

Phyllis Ginger

Right: *Design for a Wedgewood Plate with a Barrage Balloon* (Date unknown)

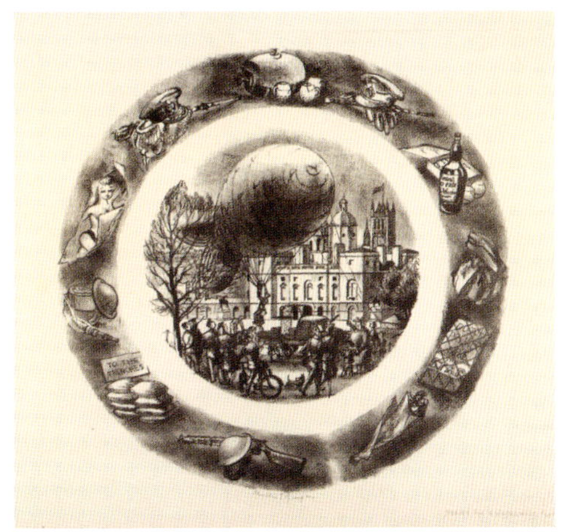

Paule Vézelay was a significant artist in the Paris avant-garde of the 1930s. She was a member of the Abstraction-Création group which included left-leaning artists such as André Masson, with whom she had a two-year relationship. Her association with such a prominent communist, as much as the abstract nature of her work, made her an object of suspicion to the authorities, who froze her out and refused her increasingly desperate pleas for a drawing permit. Returning to her home city of Bristol, she eventually obtained a permit with the support of Bristol Museum and Art Gallery. She recorded the destruction of the city centre by German bombs in drawings that, while more representational than her earlier work in France, still reflect her interest in form and composition. At the end of the war Vezélay returned to the abstract, but continued to be more highly regarded in Europe than at home in Britain. A Tate retrospective of 1983 began to restore her reputation, but she is still not as well known as she should be.

WAAC commissions and purchases from female artists on the home front tended towards subjects connected to women, children and health. This may have been a result of practical considerations – these were the subjects women artists were more likely to encounter – or may have been the result of the artists' preferences, or indeed of WAAC members' assumptions about what was appropriate. None of these factors can be completely dissociated from social expectations about women's roles at this time. The evacuation of children from British cities to protect them from bombing was covered for the WAAC by both male and female artists, but was also covered unofficially by women artists with the freedom to choose their own subjects. Ethel Gabain's series of beautifully executed lithographs, commissioned by the WAAC, promote an idealised view of evacuation, and emphasise the rural idyll to which the children had escaped. In contrast Janey Ironside, working unofficially, captures a sense of the vulnerability and displacement which many children must have experienced in her delicate pencil drawings.

Since the Second World War, without the urgent motivation of sustaining civilian morale and support, government patronage has been on a far smaller scale.[4] Artists have responded to atrocities or other mass civilian casualties of war largely from their own individual motivation, often from a standpoint of questioning the morality of conflicts or raising awareness of their consequences. Others reflect on events which involve or affect them in some way.

Paule Vézelay

Damaged Steel Girders, Bristol 1941

'My work is very modern, even in Paris. Is the committee so reactionary at the Central Institute that it is displeasing to them? That may well be so. Nevertheless, while the modern weapons and inventions are needed to win the war, it would seem to me most suitable that the most modern artists are most likely to record it in a fitting manner.'

Paule Vézelay, in a letter to the War Artists Advisory Committee in July 1941, questions the reasons for the committee's apparent reluctance to grant her a commission.

(Imperial War Museum War Artists Archive)

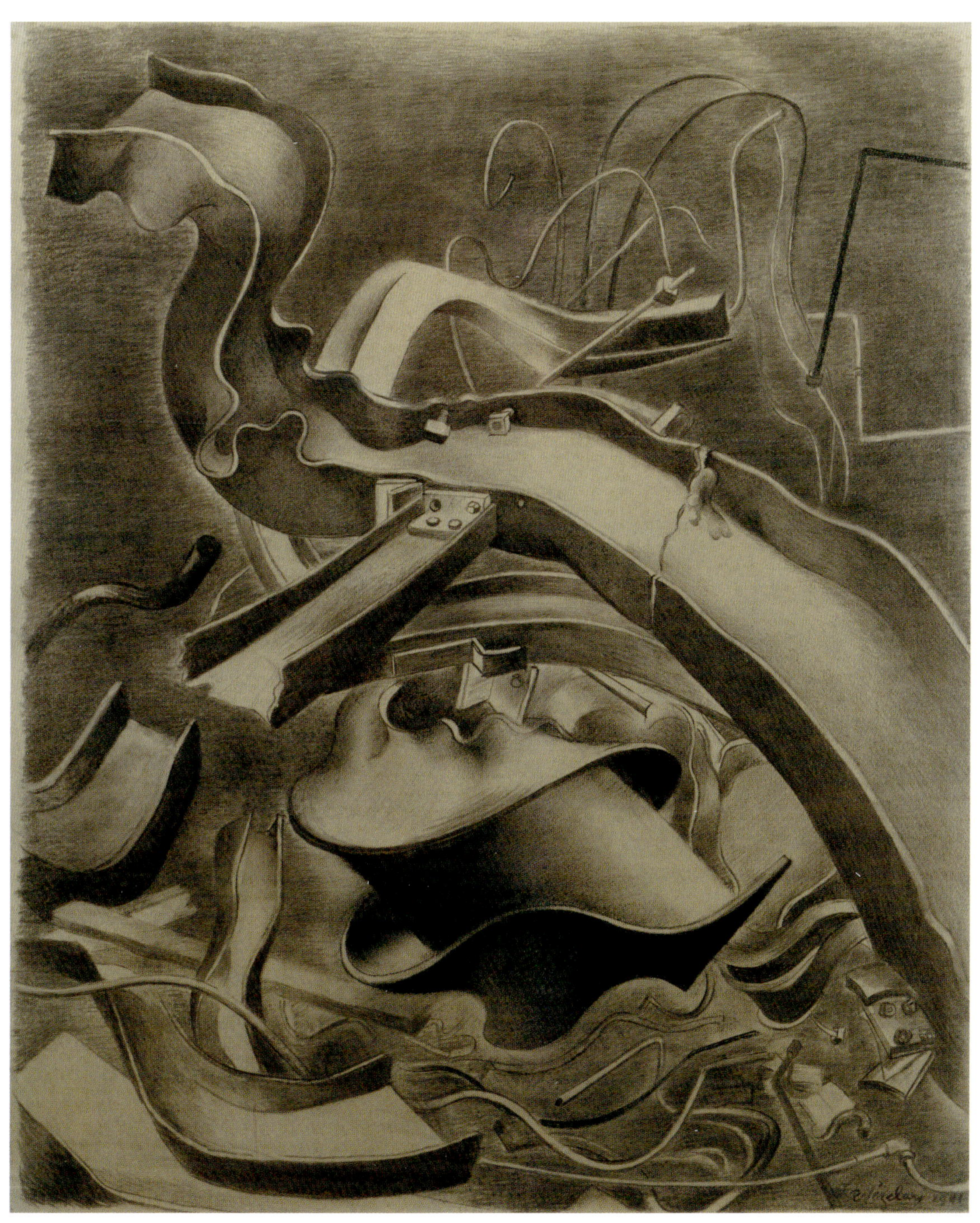

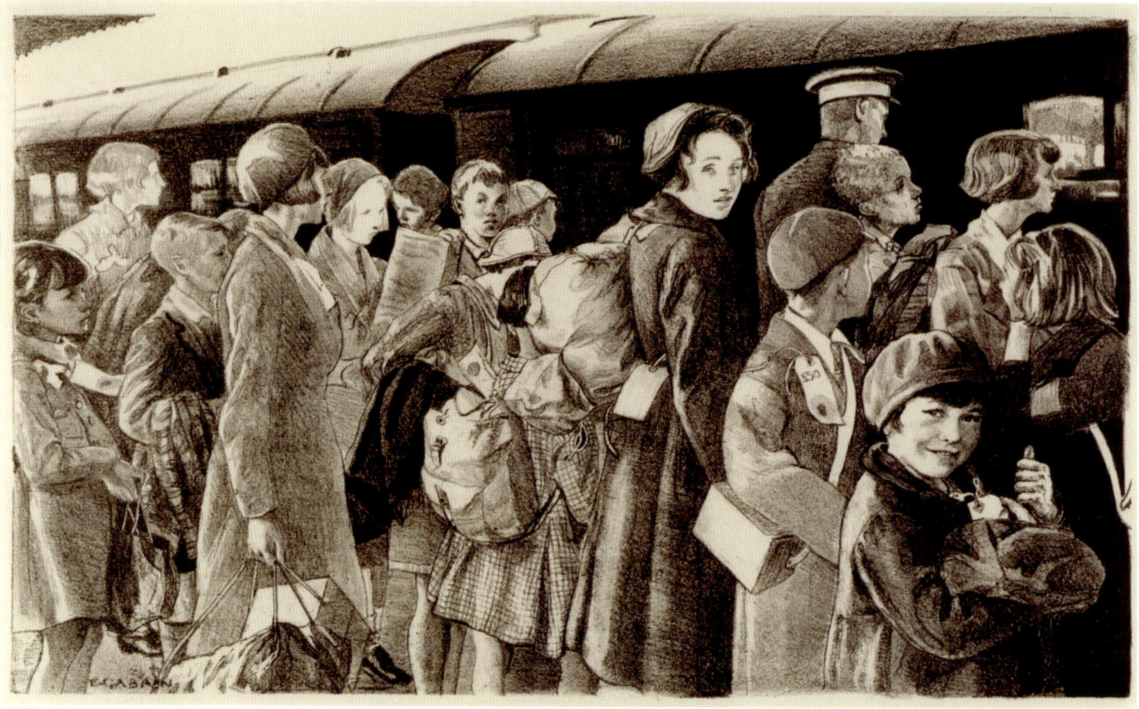

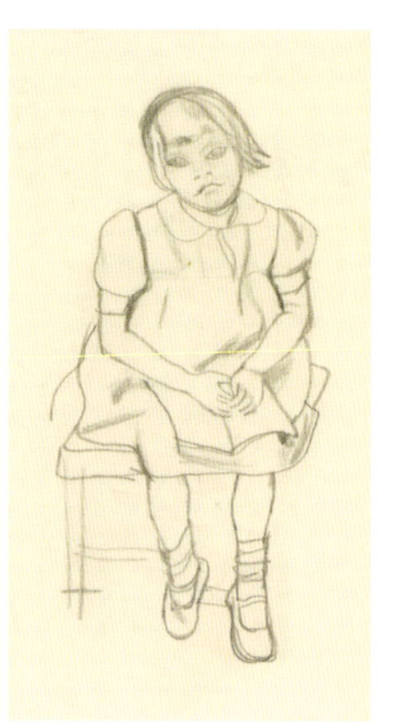

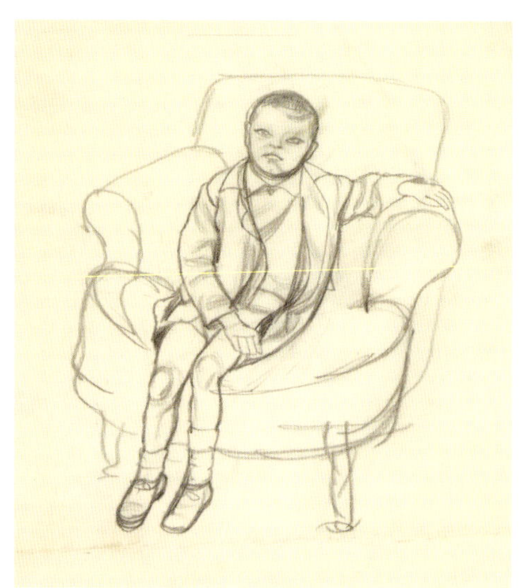

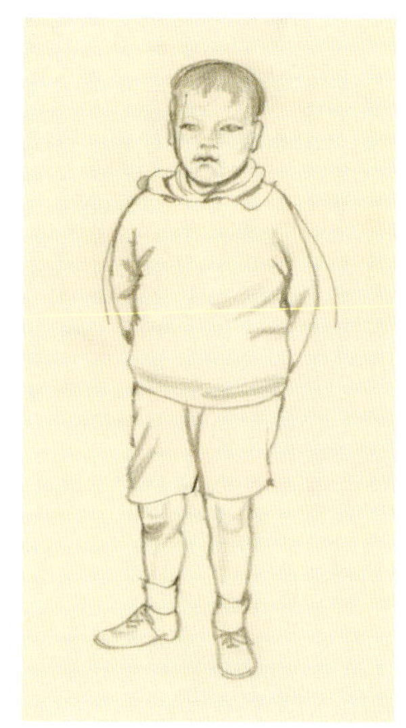

Ethel Gabain

Top left: *The Evacuation of Children from Southend* 1940

Janey Ironside

Bottom left: From the series *Evacuees in Leamington Spa* c.1940

In looking at scarred bodies, Sophie Ristelhueber's 1994 *Every One* series follows a theme within the artist's work – examining the scars and traces of war on architecture and landscape – to its logical conclusion. The work was created in response to the Bosnian War, and followed a 1991 visit to Yugoslavia at the height of the Croatian War.[5] Contrary to immediate expectations the photographs were not taken in Bosnia – these are in fact patients at a Paris hospital. The text selected for the artist's book of the series is an extract from a Classical Greek text, Thucydides' *History of the Peloponnesian War*, an account of a brutal war between the rival Greek city-states of Athens and Sparta. And so the artist creates an allusive, metaphorical comment on the Bosnian conflict, making us consider the long history of conflict in human society, and the wounds war continues to inflict on individuals and cultures.

Sophie Ristelhueber

Right: *Every One 14* 1994

Black and white photograph, silver print. 290 x 180cm.

Unique, collection Victoria & Albert Museum, London. © Sophie Ristelhueber / adagp Paris

'In the early '90s I photographed freshly operated bodies for what became **Every One** – a metaphor about the civil war in the Balkans. I did it quickly in a Paris hospital where I was looking for shapes – of stitches, cuts and wounds – that would speak clearly about the conflict.'

Sophie Ristelhueber, in a 2009 interview with Guy Lane for *Art World* magazine.

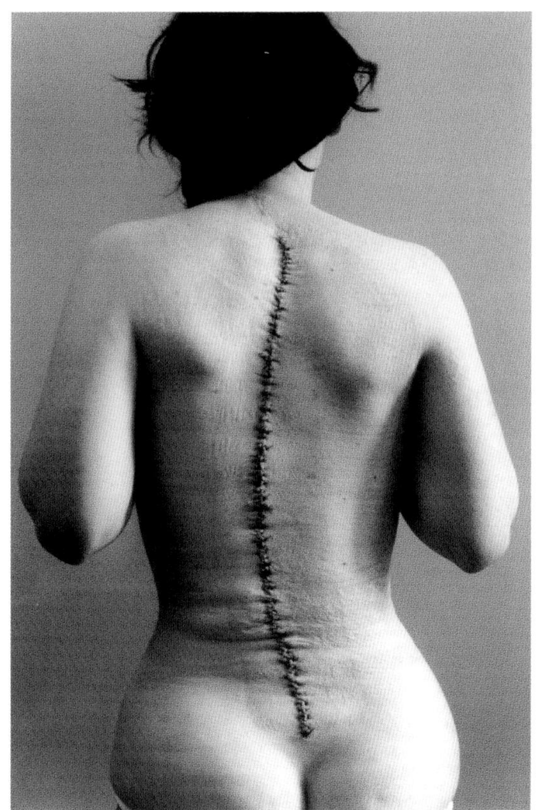

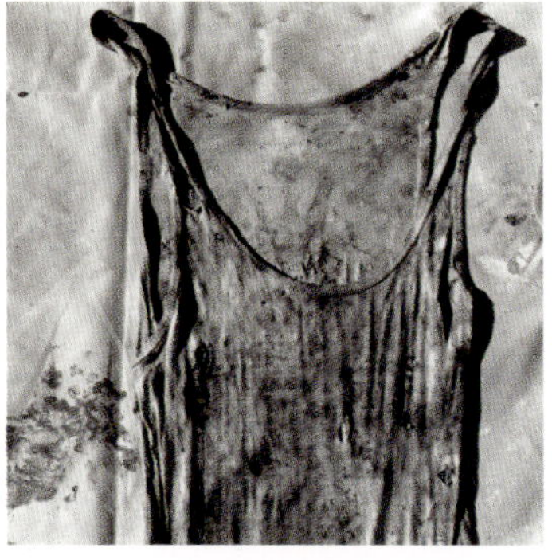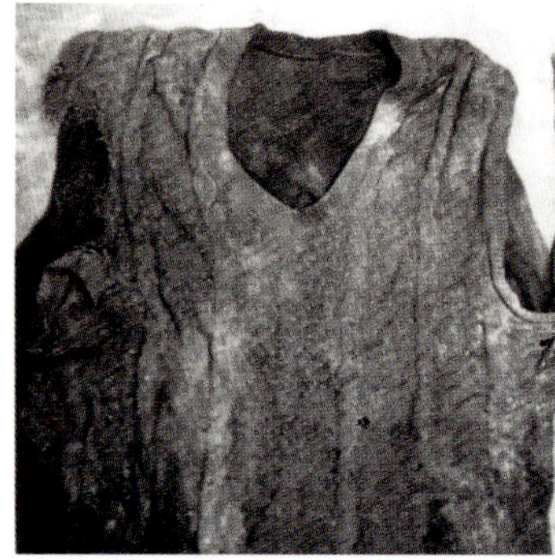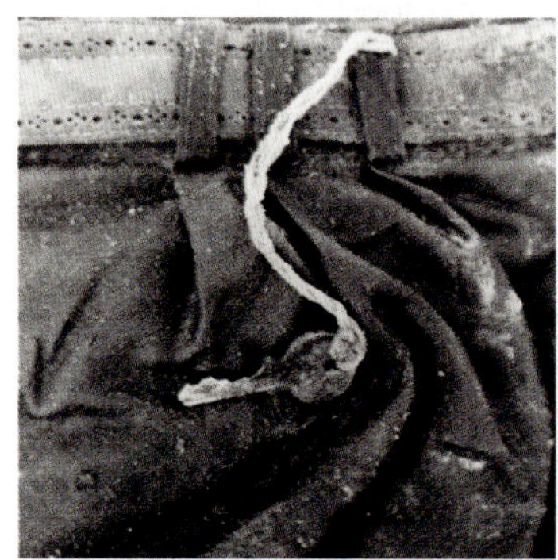

Frauke Eigen

Left: *Fundstücke Kosovo* Series
Unterhemd [Vest]
Pullunder [Sleeveless Pullover]
Uhr [Watch]
Schlüssel [Keys] 2000, 2002

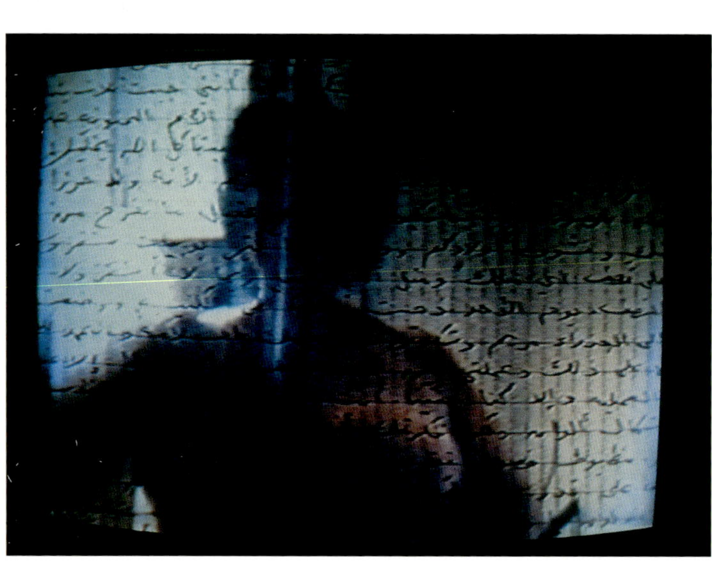

Mona Hatoum

Left: *Measures of Distance* 1988

Colour video, sound, fifteen
minutes. A Western Front Video
Production, Vancouver

© the artist
Courtesy White Cube

Frauke Eigen describes in the text of her portfolio how the photographs came about.

(Imperial War Museum)

Mona Hatoum, from a conversation with Janine Antoni, first published in *BOMB Magazine*, No. 63, Spring 1998.

In her portfolio of photographs *Fundstücke Kosovo* [*Kosovo Finds*], Frauke Eigen evokes the memory of the victims of ethnic cleansing. By photographing personal effects and clothing from bodies which had been exhumed from mass graves, Eigen prompts us to consider the terrible fate of the real people to whom they had once belonged. The artist creates resonant, thought-provoking images, without arousing immediate disgust or revulsion.

This move away from direct representation of horror to a more oblique approach is common to a whole generation of artists, including male artists such as Christian Boltanski and Alfredo Jaar, as well as female ones. The rise of journalistic and charity advertising images designed to shock the viewer has progressively reduced the impact of the artist as a recorder, as well as raising ethical concerns about exploiting victims of conflict. Artist-witnesses of mass killings are now seeking a means, through their creative responses, to allow viewers to engage their imaginations in facing horror rather than turn away.

National, Community and Personal Identities

The interaction of globalisation, contemporary conflict and gender make identity an increasingly complex area for contemporary women artists to explore. Following the end of the Cold War, there has been an upsurge in nationalism and ethnic conflict. The increasing global movement of people, whether as refugees from conflict or for other reasons, has resulted in greater cultural exchange. Artists bring more diverse perspectives to bear on conflict, responding to events in ways that are uniquely shaped by their background and experiences. Many contemporary women artists are also acutely aware of the discourses of feminist art history and conscious of their identity and position as female artists.

Mona Hatoum's early work *Measures of Distance* draws together threads of exile, separation and female identity which stem from her background in a Palestinian family living in Lebanon, and her enforced separation from her family during the Lebanese Civil War. The film shows images of the artist's mother taking a shower overlaid with text from her letters to her daughter. The artist reads the letters aloud in English, over the sound of a taped conversation in Arabic between herself and her mother. The letters cover the subject of the war, their separation, and also the opening up of a more intimate dialogue about womanhood and sexuality arising from taking the photographs during a rare visit. The interweaving of these strands serves to highlight and intensify the implications of the separation communicated to the viewer.

Born in Kirkuk to an Iraqi father and an Irish mother, Jananne Al-Ani uses her dual national identity and family relationships to examine conflict, absence, loss and displacement. *Untitled May 1991* [*Gulf War Work*] explores Al-Ani's reaction to the Gulf War (1990–1) both as a distanced observer, watching events unfold through the media, and as someone directly affected by them. The photographs show – in rows from the top – Iraqi archaeological artefacts, family photographs, formal portraits of the artist, her mother and her sisters, and media images of the conflict. The juxtaposition of images of family history and national heritage with newspaper photographs intimates the complexity of events as experienced by individuals, as opposed to the simplifications of media reporting into 'us and them', good and bad.

Al-Ani's 1996–9 video installation *A Loving Man* explores the memories the artist, her mother and her three sisters have of her father, who did not leave with them in 1980 at the start of the Iran-Iraq war. The work takes the format of a memory game, with each participant's phrase added on to the phrases which have come before. The women are all dressed in black, and each presented on a separate monitor within a darkened circular space, giving a severe formality to the work which undercuts the playfulness of the memory game device. The restricted space emphasises the interactions within the family relationship, and in an echoing dynamic forces the viewer to negotiate around the presence of others viewing the work. The multiple speakers, their hesitancy, and the varying delivery of remembered phrases create a disrupted, fragmented memory underlining the impossibility of a true narrative of the past.

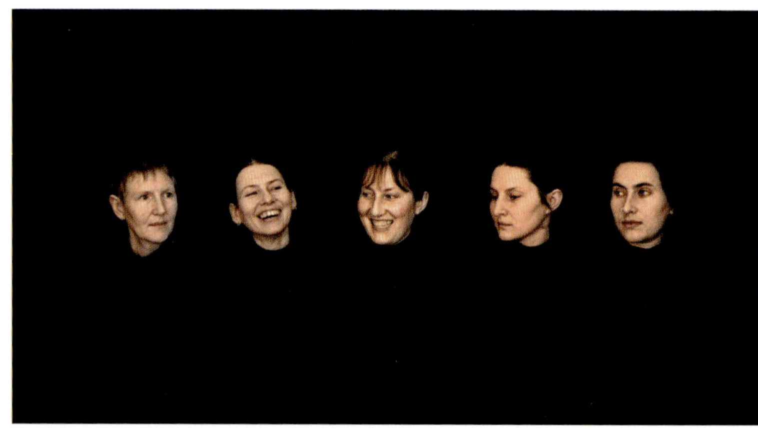

Jananne Al-Ani

Left: *A Loving Man* [Composite image derived from video] 1996–9

Courtesy the artist

Rita Duffy

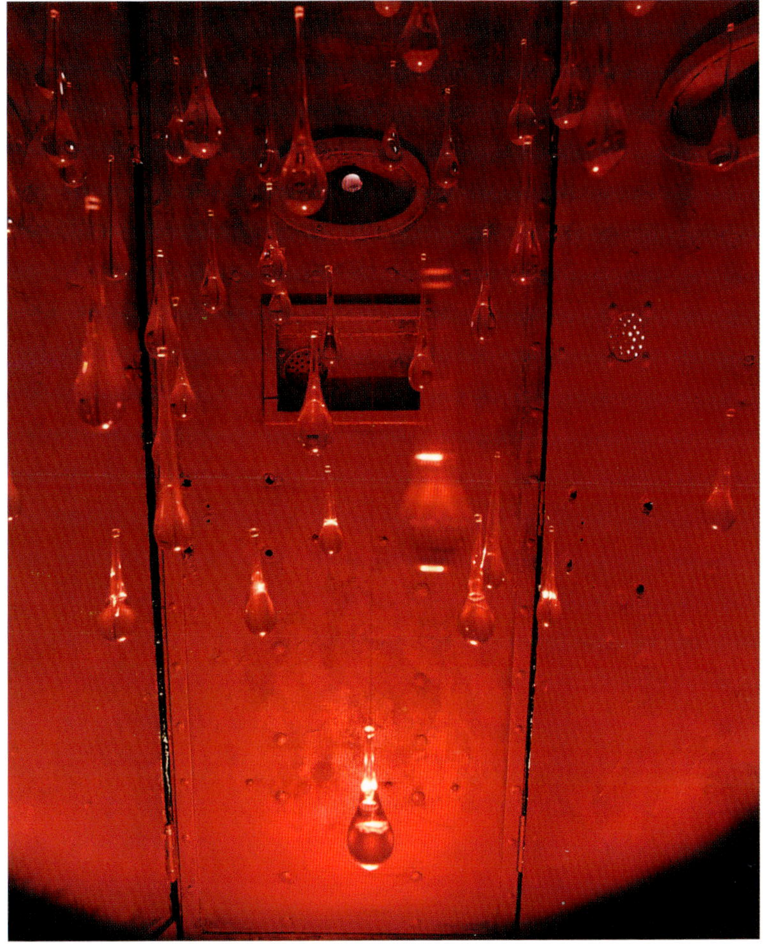

Veil by Rita Duffy also highlights an aspect of women's experiences of conflict in Northern Ireland which is often overlooked. Duffy has constructed a 'cell' from the doors of the disused Armagh Women's Prison. Viewers look through the inspection hatches in the doors to see a blood red interior, perhaps alluding to the dirty protests of female republican political prisoners, which included smearing menstrual blood on their cell walls. Eighty glass tear drops are suspended within the chamber, and a dusting of salt laid around the chamber also symbolises the tears shed by the prisoners. The piece reminds us that women were involved in the conflict in Northern Ireland as combatants and prisoners, not just as mothers, wives and daughters.

In *Allegiances and Assurances*, Sandra Johnston looks at community identity during conflict and peacetime through her experience of living in three Northern Irish Protestant communities at different times. The work is a three screen video installation: the first screen shows members of the Boys' Brigade rehearsing their drill for the annual Orange Day Parade; the centre screen focuses on spectators at a parade; and the final screen shows footage shot by Johnston in the 1990s of youths watching over the huge bonfire stacks which were an aggressive feature of these celebrations. The work reflects not only the role of tradition in demarcating sectarian territories, but also how these traditions are evolving and being reworked while remaining significant to community identity.

Smadar Dreyfus explores the voice, its presence and effect in contested public spaces, and its implication in the negotiation of cultural perspective. A native of Israel, now based in London, Dreyfus often examines aspects of society in Israel in her work. For her 2008 immersive installation *Mother's Day* the artist recorded sound at the annual Syrian 'Mother's Day' event at the Israeli-Syrian ceasefire line in the Golan Heights. Druze mothers on the Israeli-controlled side exchange greetings with their student sons and daughters, who travel from Damascus to a place known as the 'Shouting Hill' on the Syrian side. The voices enact the border line and embody the separation through their strained attempts at intimacy over a public sound system. These private exchanges are subject to observation both from the media, and by Israeli, Syrian and UN forces positioned on the surrounding hilltops. Filmed images of the hill shrouded with early morning fog are shown in complete silence, alternating with sequences of immersive audio during which the words of the dialogue are projected, synchronising perfectly with the voices, in the pitch black installation space. This disjunction of sound and image throws into sharp contrast the sublime landscape and the difficult situation made apparent through the voices.

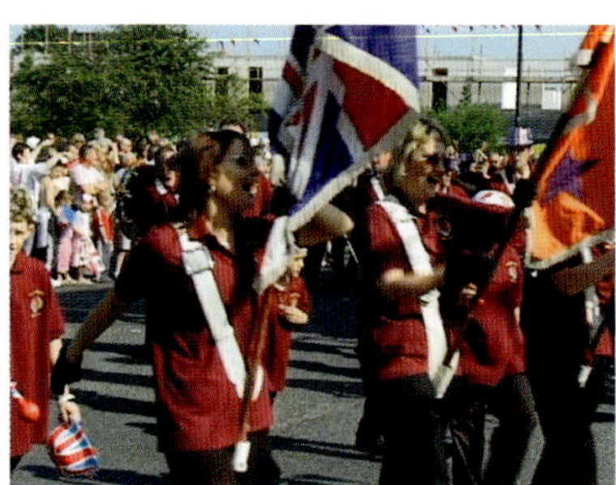

Sandra Johnston

Left: *Allegiances and Assurances* [Film still] 2008

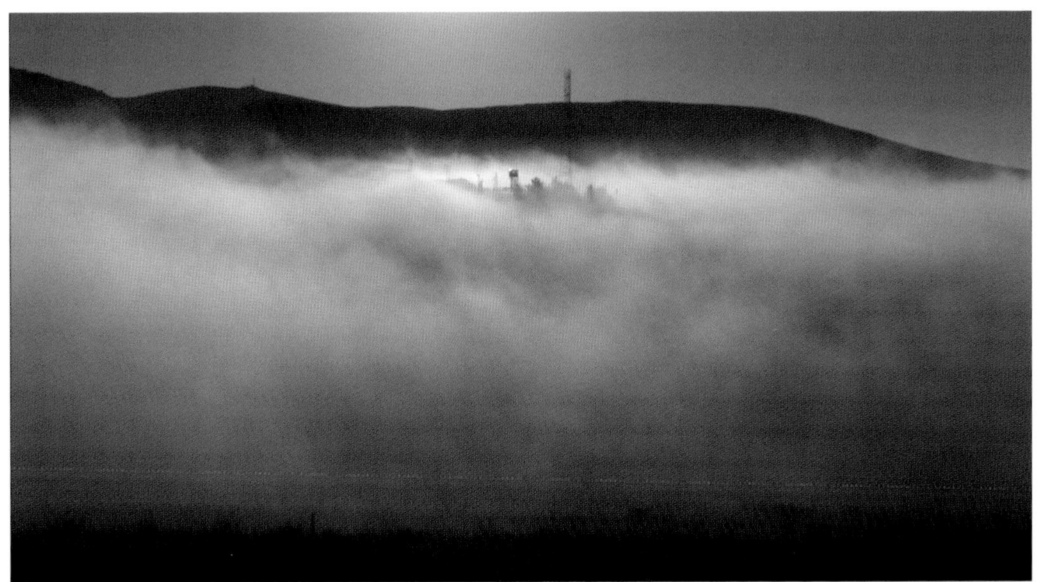

Smadar Dreyfus

Above: *Mother's Day* [Stills from video] 2006–8

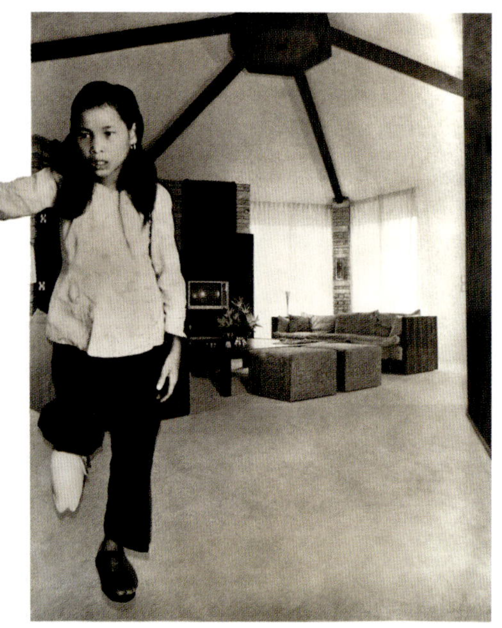

Martha Rosler

Left: *Tron (Amputee)* from the series *House Beautiful: Bringing The War Home (1967–1972)*

Courtesy the artist and Galerie Christian Nagel

Goshka Macuga

Below: *The Nature of the Beast* 2009. Installation view, The Bloomberg Commission, Whitechapel Gallery.

Courtesy Whitechapel Gallery and Kate MacGarry, London. Photo: Patrick Lears.

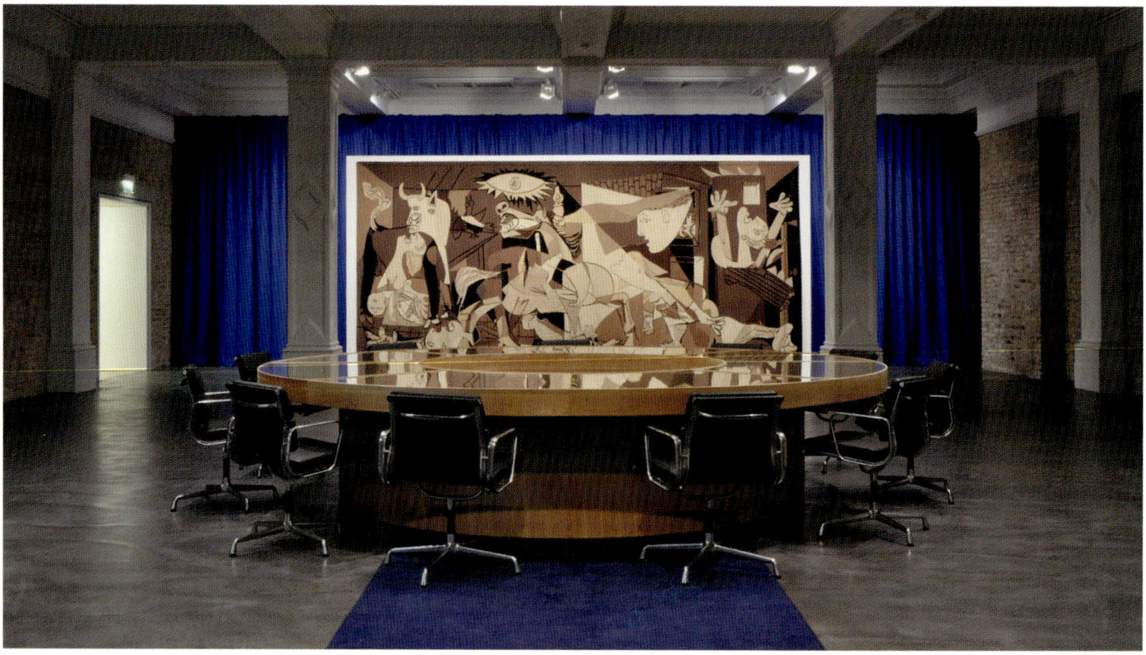

Morality, Memorial and Memory

Responses to conflict do not come only from eye witnesses or personal experiences, but also from thoughtful, creative analysis of war. Artists may choose to explore the moral complexities of war or develop a more political response. They may investigate memory, personal history or identity in the context of conflicts involving their society – both in the present and the past. Indeed artists play a key role in how society remembers and comes to terms with past conflicts. Memory, memorial and remembering are significant themes in war art. Drawing on feminist explorations of women's history, female artists have also sought to explore the experiences of women in conflicts past and present.

Martha Rosler's photomontage series *Bringing the War Home 1967–1972* powerfully challenges the morality of the Vietnam War through its exploration of the consumption of a distant war through television. The series makes a direct connection between the idealised view of American life in advertising and the suffering inflicted on civilians by American troops abroad – Rosler saw the two worlds represented entirely separately within the pages of *Life* magazine, and felt that the connection between them must be made explicit. In common with British contemporaries such as Peter Kennard and Richard Hamilton, Rosler's work has its roots in the Dadaist use of photomontage for political and feminist purposes by artists such as John Heartfield and Hannah Höch. Rosler has returned to the medium of photomontage since 2000 in response to America's involvement in Afghanistan and Iraq, feeling that this reprise would underline the similarity of past and present conflicts and her critical message in opposing them.

Goshka Macuga's 2009 *Nature of the Beast* installation at the Whitechapel Art Gallery connects the exhibition of Picasso's *Guernica* at the gallery towards the end of the Spanish Civil War in 1939 with the current political context of the conflict in Iraq.[6] Archive documents illustrate the context and politics of the 1939 exhibition, and the painting itself is represented by its tapestry copy on loan from the United Nations Headquarters. Shown alongside is hard-hitting anti-war film footage questioning the moral justification of the Iraq War and its impact on Iraqi civilians, intermingled with pro-Republican film footage from the Spanish Civil War. A cubist-style sculpture of former US Secretary of State Colin Powell highlights references to the controversial covering of the *Guernica* tapestry at the UN – during the press conference which followed Powell's speech advocating the invasion of Iraq on 5 February 2003, the

Kathleen Scott

Right: *The Thinking Soldier*
(Huntingdon War Memorial)
1923

Courtesy of Jennifer Sarabia

Maya Lin

Bottom left: Vietnam Veterans'
Memorial. Competition drawing
c.1980

Bottom right: Vietnam Veterans'
Memorial at Washington DC

© L Clarke/Corbis

tapestry was covered by a blue curtain. Macuga's complex interplay of historical and contemporary is a subtle and layered investigation of the morality of war and the nature of the artist's political role in addressing conflict.

Only a tiny handful of war memorials built in Britain after the First World War were sculpted or designed by women. Female sculptors were more successful in securing commissions for portrait busts rather than monumental public sculpture. A rare exception is Kathleen Scott's memorial for Market Hill, Huntingdon, *The Thinking Soldier*. This well-executed and moving sculpture of a contemplative Tommy shows the influence of her teacher Rodin's famous work, *The Thinker*. Scott was both gifted and socially adept, and during her career created many portraits of influential politicians and leading literary figures. She is perhaps best known for her sculpture of her late husband, the explorer Robert Falcon Scott ('Scott of the Antarctic').

Few new memorials were commissioned following the Second World War; in most cases new names were added to existing ones. One of the best known post-war public monuments designed by a woman is Maya Lin's iconic 1982 Vietnam National War Memorial in Washington DC. Lin won the commission through an anonymous open competition while still a student. Its minimalist architecture was controversial at first, although the memorial is now widely admired. Lin's concept was to create a cut in the earth, like a wound, symbolising the pain of loss, but also the beginning of healing. The black polished stone was deliberately chosen for its reflective quality, to join past and present by showing the living reflected alongside the names of the dead.

First commissioned in 1996, Rachel Whiteread's Holocaust Memorial in Vienna was unveiled in 2000 after years of obstructions and controversy. The work takes the form of an inaccessible room walled with shelves of identical books. The room has been inverted in curious ways: the books are visible on the outside, showing their closed pages rather than their spines; a ceiling rose projects from the roof. The double doors have no handles, denying access and emphasising the library as forever closed and unreadable. This conceptual piece has layers of possible interpretations and references: to the 'People of the Book'; to Nazi book burning; to the rich cultural contribution made by Austrian Jews; or to the untold individual stories of those who were killed. Like Maya Lin's Vietnam Veterans' Memorial, or indeed the Cenotaph in Whitehall, it is also a powerful demonstration of the fact that art does not need to be literal and figurative in order to memorialise war or genocide.

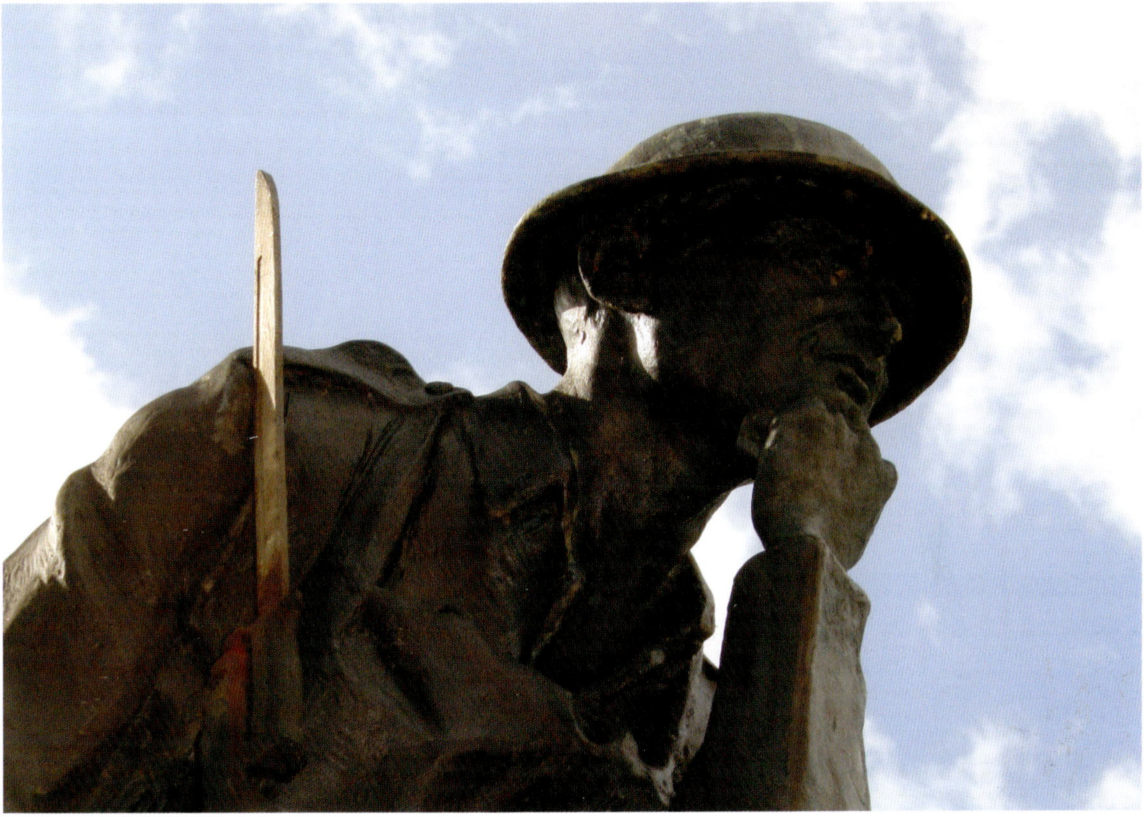

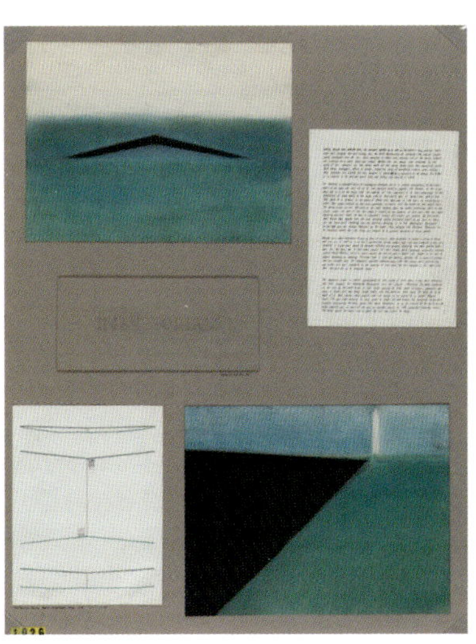

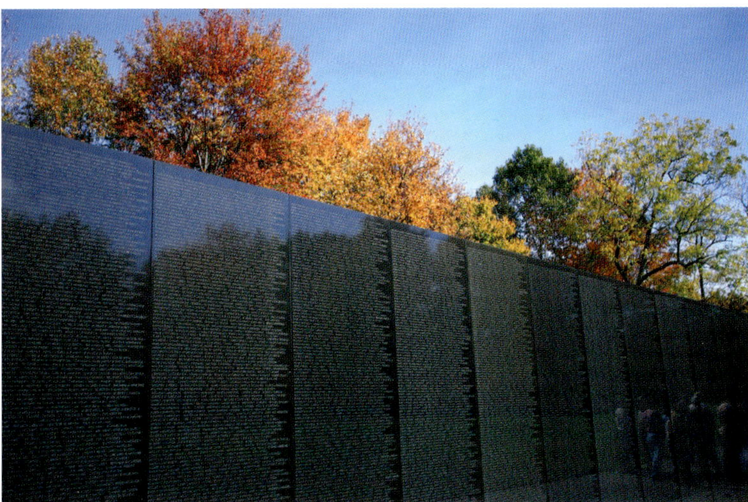

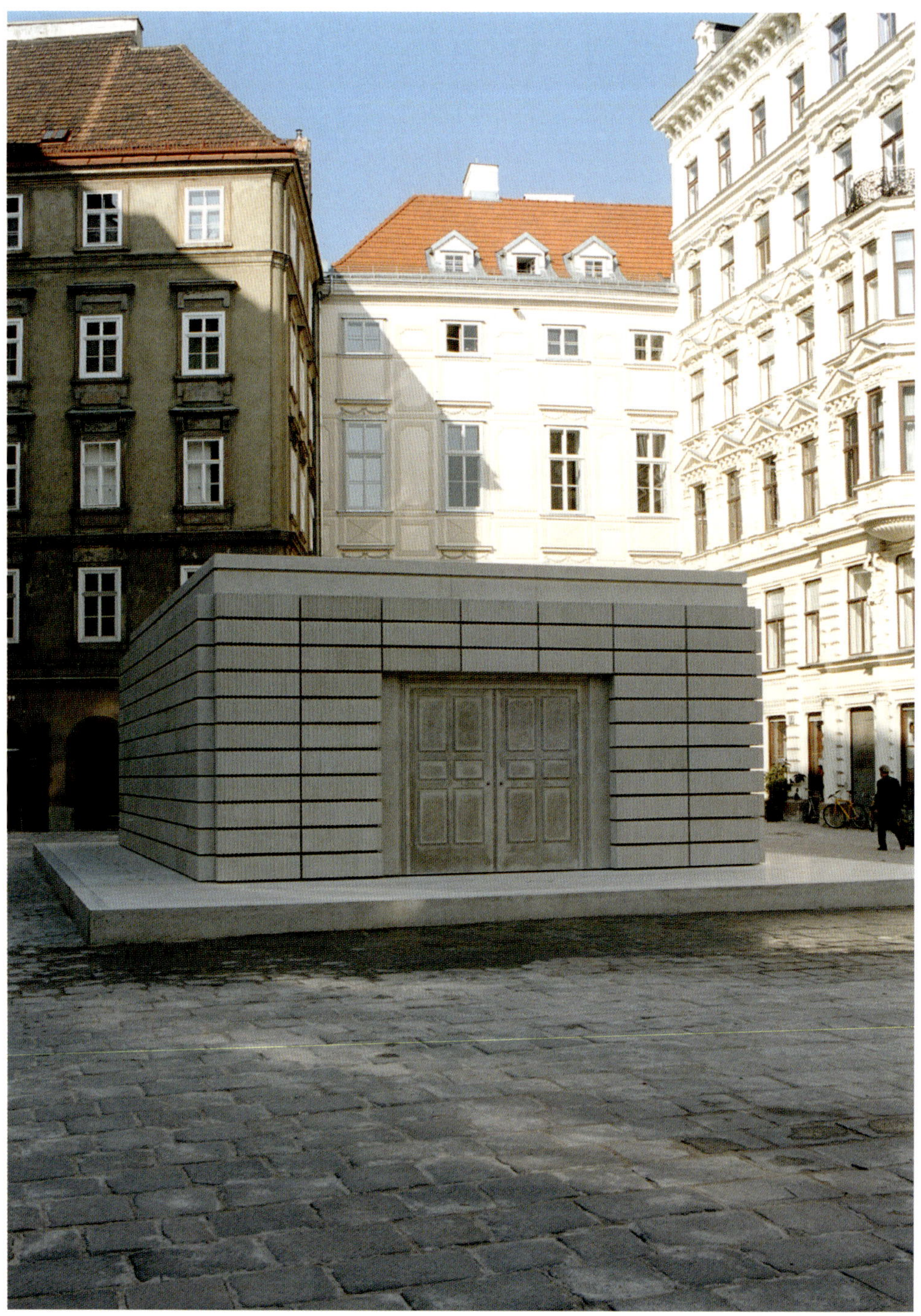

The Costs of War | Morality, Memorial and Memory

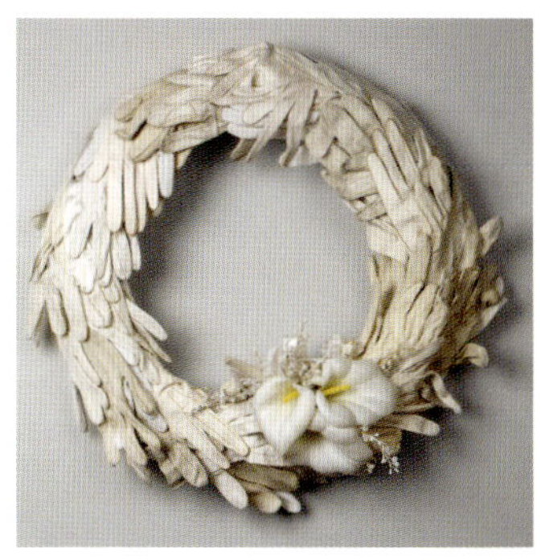

Rozanne Hawksley

Above: *Pale Armistice* 1991

Rachel Whiteread

Left: Holocaust Memorial,
1995/2000
Judenplatz Vienna

Mixed Media
390 x 752 x 1058 cm

Courtesy of the artist, Luhring
Augustine, New York and
Gagosian Gallery

Themes of memorial, family history and the morality of war are interwoven in Rozanne Hawksley's *Pale Armistice*. A funeral wreath made from overlapped white gloves with artificial white flowers and found bleached bones, it articulates the hidden suffering of women bereaved in the First World War. The work was created in memory of the artist's grandmother. Through the 'feminine' medium of textile and stitching the artist points to the need for an exploration of the past as experienced by women. Works such as Rozsika Parker's 1984 book *The Subversive Stitch* have been influential in changing attitudes to sewing and embroidery, challenging the historic under-valuing of women's artistic outputs and critically re-evaluating the medium and its place in women's social interaction.

The work of Susan Philipsz is primarily about memory and place, using songs to evoke the memories embodied in particular places. The songs, sung by the artist unaccompanied, are introduced to the spaces in unexpected and deliberately low-fi ways, such as through public address systems. *From a Distance* is a permanent, site-specific work created for AirSpace at Imperial War Museum Duxford in 2009, through the Museum's Art Commissions Committee. Finding the wide open spaces of the historic airfield redolent of watching and waiting for the safe return of an aircraft, Philipsz chose to sing The Jam's 'English Rose': 'No matter where I roam I will return to my English rose'. While the song plays a scrolling list of the aircraft on display is projected, and the whole work is played following on from the general introductory film for AirSpace.

[1] The most well-known example is the censorship of C.R.W. Nevinson's *Paths of Glory* which he then proceeded to exhibit covered with a band marked 'CENSORED', thus generating enormous publicity.

[2] Ulrike Smalley, 'Objective Realists – British War Artists as Witnesses to the Liberation of Bergen-Belsen Concentration Camp', *The Holocaust in History and Memory*, vol. 2, 2009, pp.53–67.

[3] Val Williams, *Warworks – Women, Photography and the Iconography of War*, London 1994, pp.35–38.

[4] In the absence of such grave conflict there has not been the motivation to support war art to such a significant extent, or the possibility of public support for a Ministry of Information tasked with shaping public opinion in a democratic society. Commissioning of official war art has continued solely under the auspices of the Imperial War Museum.

[5] First exhibited at the Centraal Museum, Utrecht, March 1994. Later that year the artist also exhibited one image from the series along with copies of *Fait* at the Obala Arts Centre, Sarajevo, during the siege of the city.

[6] This was a political act to garner support for the Spanish Republican cause, hosted by the Whitechapel Art Gallery in response to a request from the Stepney Trades Union Council.

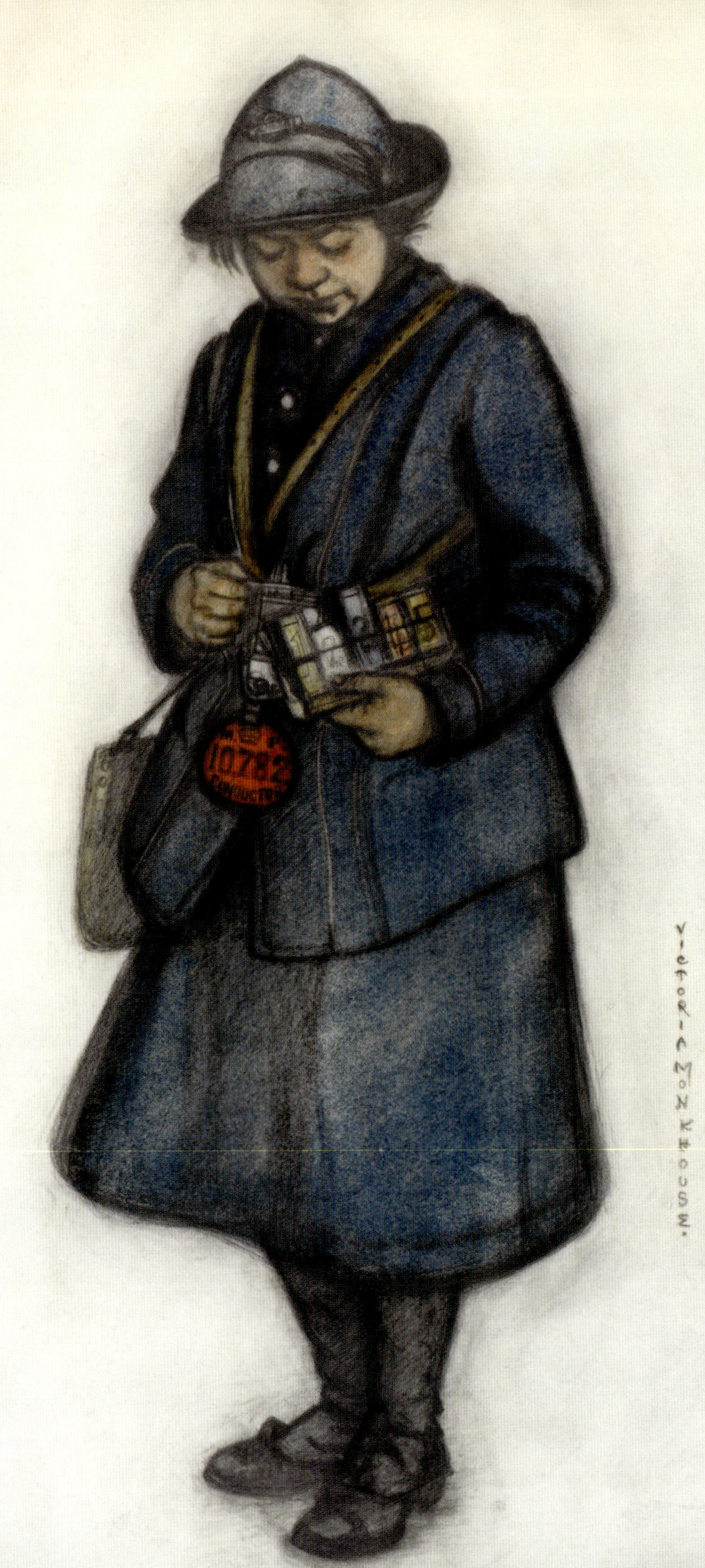

Afterword: Women as War Artists

Women artists are as equally drawn to the subject of war as their male counterparts, but have simply not enjoyed the same opportunities or reputation. It is important to assess the output of women war artists in the context of the differences in the opportunities offered to them. It would be easy to assume a bias amongst female artists towards subjects such as women, children, domestic and caring work, but, during the two World Wars, this was simply the nature of the commissions on offer to them. Even within the small selection of women war artists considered in this book it is clear that women artists follow many paths of artistic enquiry and approach all aspects of war – from weapons, architecture or geography to themes of memory, time and perception. In examining their work what emerges most strongly is its huge diversity.

Looking at women artists separately risks isolating them from the mainstream, or reinforcing generalisations. Yet female artists are part of the artistic culture of an age; they influence and are influenced by peers, critics, teachers and students. These connections to particular artistic trends or artistic sources and influences and comparisons with the work of their male colleagues are important in placing them within the context of broader art historical narratives. There is no generic characteristic in women's war art, no unusual capacity for empathy, but much that is individual, innovative and exciting emerges in the range of subjects and approaches shown here.

Amongst the most enduring and popular images by women war artists of the two World Wars are those in which they show other women adapting to the demands of wartime. They create heroines of individual women, or anonymous women workers, seemingly supporting many of the assumptions of their times about gender roles and women's capabilities. The subjects of these paintings mirror the artists' own position as female war workers in the artistic field, making their way within the constraints of a male-dominated society.

In the portraiture officially acquired during these conflicts a rich variety of approaches and styles can be seen. Olive Edis's unusual use of only natural light in her photographic portraits gives them a great sense of candour. Clare Atwood's soft and delicate brushstrokes build up a warm vibrancy in her skilfully composed group portrait. The soft finish of Victoria Monkhouse's watercolours emphasises the femininity of her subjects, whilst Dame Laura Knight's bold realism matches the heroism of her sitters (both male and female) and reflects her own strong character. In *The Nuremberg Trial* Knight achieves her most intense statement, her meticulous

Victoria Monkhouse

A Bus Conductress 1919

portraits of the defendants contrasting with the dream-like quality of the ruined city in the background. Ethel Gabain's unpretentious, informal portrait of Alexander Fleming shows the great scientist at work in his laboratory, while the shading and texture in her lithographs of evacuees display assured mastery of the technique.

A similar diversity emerges in the field of war reportage, some works forming almost an illustrated diary of experiences in the war zone, others capturing observed details. Olive Mudie-Cooke delivers a series of versatile and accomplished drawings, and might have become better known if it were not for her early suicide. Mary Kessell's vigorous drawings evoke empathy for the plight of the German people in the aftermath of the Allied victory. Stella Schmolle shows her skill as an illustrator in capturing telling incidents from her ATS training and service overseas. Following very consciously in the tradition of Second World War reportage, Linda Kitson was strongly influenced by male war artists such as Edward Bawden.

Although some of these women war artists are not now so well known, the recognition which they enjoyed in their own lifetimes should not be underestimated. Many of the female artists commissioned after the First World War by the Women's Work Sub-committee (WWS) enjoyed great success during the Edwardian period and beyond. Anna Airy, Flora Lion, Clare Atwood and Lucy Kemp-Welch were all highly respected artists, elected as members of prestigious artistic societies such as the Royal Institute of Oil Painters and the Royal Society of Portrait Painters. They exhibited at the Royal Academy, or in Atwood's case with the New English Art Club. Norah Neilson-Gray was one of the 'Glasgow Girls', a group of successful women artists teaching at Glasgow School of Art. All were affected by a subsequent decline in the reputation of Edwardian painting, which also eclipsed all but the most outstanding of their male peers. Only very recently have these artists begun to be re-evaluated.

Laura Knight was already establishing a growing reputation during the First World War, and was considered by the Ministry of Information at this time, although never commissioned. By the time Knight worked for the War Artists Advisory Committee (WAAC) during the Second World War her reputation was very high; she was made a Dame of the British Empire in 1929, and in 1936 was the first woman in over 150 years to be elected a Royal Academician (since the founding members in 1768). Paule Vézelay enjoyed great success as part of the Parisian avant-garde of the 1930s, although her career was damaged by her enforced return to England at the outbreak of war. With her innovative and original style, Evelyn

Dunbar was developing a reputation as a leading female modernist. Doris Zinkeisen was forging a very successful career in stage and film design, as well as working in other fields of design and painting. Of these only Laura Knight has subsequently remained well-known, her realism remaining steadfastly popular while the more modernist figurative painters were overshadowed by the primacy of abstract art.

Even where no official commission was in place or any official purchase likely, women artists chose to engage with both world wars. Lucy Kemp-Welch and others were successful during the First World War with traditional battle paintings. By the Second World War a much wider range of women were making a living as artists. Many of those who did not secure government patronage on any large scale nevertheless chose to respond to the war and to use their artistic skills for the war effort. Like the male soldier artists who worked outside of the official schemes, their work offers an unvarnished response to their wartime experience. Works such as Priscilla Thornycroft's deliberately address the working class experience of war. In Margaret Abbess's factory drawings, the interaction between the sexes is intriguingly different from that shown in official war art.

Contemporary artists largely take a more conceptual approach, explicitly examining ideas and values. Some female artists challenge society's current gender relationships or seek to unravel their complexities by exploring the experiences of women past and present. Sandra Johnston's work evokes issues of how women participate in conflict in Northern Ireland, not only as observers, but also as supporters and facilitators. Rita Duffy deliberately draws attention to women's active presence in the Northern Irish conflict. Mona Hatoum and Jananne Al-Ani use images of women in a self-aware and considered way, particularly in involving family members. These artists have explored and thought deeply about feminist issues, including the depiction of the female body, and bring this to bear on their work. Choosing to address their own gender and place in society in a range of different ways, they respond uniquely to the challenges and opportunities it offers them.

Of course female artists are not limited to addressing gender or areas typified as female concerns. In addressing war's consequences for individuals and communities, and the need for commemoration and remembering, women artists respond primarily as individuals. Their approaches are diverse and varied, and draw on the same wide range of artistic and personal influences which also shape their male counterparts. Sophie Ristelhueber's use of the destruction of architecture and landscape as a metaphor to express human suffering has its roots historically in the eighteenth century Romantic movement and the concept of the sublime, traceable through the work of First World War artists such as Paul Nash, and is part of a wider trend in contemporary art. Martha Rosler and Goshka Macuga find means to question the morality of particular conflicts, with the strong contrasts embedded in Rosler's photomontages clearly making a direct protest, while Macuga builds up historical references to direct questioning of contemporary events. The meaning and purpose of weapons are thrown into question through the works of Fiona Banner, Mona Hatoum and Rita Duffy.

Contemporary artists have adopted many new media over the past two decades, and women artists have often been in the forefront, taking forward use of film and video, sound installation, performance and the use of craft media such as textiles. Nikki Bell and Ben Langlands have used a wide range of media to create subtle, complex conceptual responses to geopolitics and global patterns of communication and exchange, including film, sculpture, print, textile and architecture. Sound is used by Smadar Dreyfus to immerse and implicate the audience in the experience of culturally contested public spaces, while Susan Philipsz uses it in an intangible, Proustian evocation of memory. Rozanne Hawksley's influential textile works mix memorial, memory and the corporeal and emotional effects of war. Rachel Whiteread's Holocaust Memorial contributes to the development of a contemporary, minimalist language of commemoration which avoids sentimentality or banality for more complex, allusive forms.

Attitudes to women have changed enormously since the First World War, and women artists now operate in a very different climate. There is far greater acknowledgement of their achievements, and they enjoy a much higher profile through increased representation in public collections, exhibitions, critical writing and the art market. Understanding the history of women as artists, and rediscovering and re-evaluating their work has been important in opening up debates and establishing role models. Highlighting the history and place of women as war artists is intended to contribute to this process.

Artists' Biographies

This is not a comprehensive account of all the artists featured in this book, but rather an attempt to supply some details of the lives of those for whom such information is not readily available in published or online sources, or where the Imperial War Museum's archives can add useful detail.

Researched and written by Sara Bevan and Amanda Mason.

Margaret Abbess (1922–2008)

At the outbreak of war in 1939 Margaret Abbess moved with her family from Leytonstone, London, to Devon. She studied at art college in Newton Abbot before returning to London. Abbess was offered a place at the Royal College of Art (RCA) but was conscripted into war work in 1942.

Security was extremely tight in factories engaged in war production. Drawing sensitive subjects or places required a permit – which Abbess did not have. Nonetheless, while working in an aircraft components factory she produced several drawings of factory scenes. This work was produced in secret, often during breaks, and provides a unique and unofficial insight into factory life. Most of Abbess's drawings began as small sketches which she later completed at home from memory.

After the war, Abbess finished her studies at the RCA and worked for many years in art education. She kept her war drawings but felt they were of limited artistic value. In 2005 she considered destroying them, but was encouraged by her family to offer them to the Imperial War Museum.

Anna Airy (1882–1964)

Anna Airy was one of the first women to be officially commissioned as a war artist. Trained at the Slade School of Fine Art, she was a gifted painter in oil and watercolour as well as an etcher, and she exhibited work at the Royal Academy (RA) throughout her career.

Airy was commissioned by the Munitions Committee of the Imperial War Museum in June 1918 to produce four pictures, 'representing typical scenes in the following four munitions factories ... the shell forge at the National Projectile Factory, Hackney Marshes, the shell filling department at the National Shell Filling Factory, Chilwell, near Nottingham, the gun forge at the works at Openshaw near Manchester and the aircraft assembly shop at Armstrong-Whitworth, Hendon'. The subject of the Chilwell factory was eventually replaced by the Singer factory in Glasgow. The agreement under which Airy worked was unusually stringent and included penalty clauses for any delay.

Another of her paintings, showing munitions girls leaving work, was produced at the request of the Ministry of Information's British War Memorials Committee in 1919. It was rejected by the Committee and later destroyed by the artist.

Victorine Foot (1920–2000)

Born in Pembury, Kent, Victorine Foot was studying at the Central School of Arts and Crafts when it was evacuated to Northampton in 1941. During this time it was suggested that she applied for a position at the Directorate of Camouflage at Leamington Spa. Foot interrupted her studies to take up a position as a Junior Technical Assistant in the Naval Section, where she was responsible for drawing up camouflage plans from experimental ship models.

In 1943 the War Artists Advisory Committee (WAAC) acquired one of her paintings, *Camouflaging a Cruiser in Dock*, painted at Plymouth Docks. A further fifteen drawings showing life at the camouflage unit were acquired by the Imperial War Museum in 1994.

After the war Foot studied briefly at Chelsea School of Art, later moving to Edinburgh College of Art in 1946, when she married the sculptor Eric Schilsky, whom she had met at the Camouflage Unit. She later taught art in Edinburgh and exhibited widely. Her work is held in several Scottish collections, including the Scottish Arts Council Collection and Aberdeen Art Gallery.

Eleanor (Erlund) Hudson (b.1912)

Eleanor (Erlund) Hudson was born in South Devon and trained at the Royal College of Art (RCA) during the 1930s. After leaving college she travelled in northern Italy, having been awarded an RCA travelling scholarship in 1938–9. Hudson returned to Britain only two weeks before the outbreak of war in

September 1939. Unable to join the services or take up active war work due to a childhood spinal injury, Hudson went to stay with her brother near Leicester, travelling in to the city to help out in canteens and to pack prisoner of war bundles. She continued to draw, focusing on local women engaged in voluntary work.

Hudson was never commissioned as an official war artist, but at the recommendation of a former tutor she sent examples of her work to the War Artists Advisory Committee (WAAC), who purchased six of her drawings. In 1944 Hudson moved to London and worked as a driver of mobile canteens, supporting rescue parties sent to bomb sites. After the war she began to design stage sets for the ballet and became known for her delicate studies of dancers.

Janey Ironside (1919–1979)

Janey Ironside was born in 1919 and trained at the Central School of Arts and Crafts. While living in Leamington Spa during the Second World War she visited evacuees recovering in a convalescent home in the town. Later, when the children were well again, some would come to visit her in her home. It was on these occasions that she produced over forty delicate pencil and watercolour studies of these vulnerable children.

In 1956 Ironside was appointed Professor of Fashion at the Royal College of Art (RCA), teaching numerous outstanding students who became renowned designers in their own right. After leaving the RCA in 1968 she wrote several books on fashion and her autobiography *Janey* was published in 1968. A number of studies of evacuee children were presented to the Imperial War Museum by her daughter, Virginia Ironside, in 1981.

Pegaret Keeling (1915–2000)

Pegaret Keeling studied the history of dress at the Central School of Arts and Crafts from 1934–8. In 1942 she contacted the Ministry of Information (MOI), offering to produce drawings of war workers. On the recommendation of the War Artists Advisory Committee (WAAC), the MOI purchased two drawings from her in June 1943.

Keeling also produced a large series of drawings showing people at work making uniforms in clothing factories – a subject that she suggested herself – requesting assistance in obtaining the necessary permits. This subject matter apparently did not appeal to the WAAC and none of these drawings were purchased at the time. However in 2002 the Imperial War Museum purchased fourteen works by Keeling, the majority depicting scenes of uniform production.

After the war Keeling (later Pegaret Anthony) worked for over forty years as a lecturer in Historical Costume and Theatre Design at both Central St Martins and Motley School of Theatre Design, and was noted for her innovative teaching techniques.

Linda Kitson (b.1945)

Linda Kitson studied at St Martins School of Art and the Royal College of Art (RCA) where she specialised in illustration. She then taught at Camberwell, Chelsea and the City and Guilds Art Schools.

Drawings of life at *The Times* newspaper won her the Falklands commission from the Artistic Records Committee of the Imperial War Museum. Kitson became the first official female war artist to accompany troops into action during the Falklands War in 1982. She travelled on the civilian ships, which were requisitioned by the Navy, as women were not permitted on naval vessels at the time. The original intention was for Kitson to disembark at Ascension Island, but instead she stayed with the forces throughout the conflict. Kitson produced over 400 drawings showing all aspects of the war except the actual fighting, most of which occurred at night. Her drawings were often completed at speed in hostile conditions. Kitson's most impressive and effective works are those recording the daily life and difficult conditions endured by the men who took part in the conflict.

Flora Lion (1878–1958)

Flora Lion trained at St John's Wood School of Art and the Royal Academy Schools and also studied in Paris. She exhibited her work at the Royal Academy (RA) from 1900 and during a long career also produced landscapes, murals and lithographs.

Lion, an established society portrait artist, was commissioned by the Ministry of Information (MOI) to complete two large paintings showing factory scenes during the First World War. She was given special access to factories in Leeds and Bradford to produce the works. Both paintings were completed in 1918 and offered to the Imperial War Museum for a price of 150 guineas each. However, for reasons that remain unclear, the Museum did not buy either of the paintings. A note in the Museum's archives states, 'Seen by committee but not purchased, returned'. They were eventually donated to the Museum in 1927.

Victoria Monkhouse (?1883–19??)

Victoria Monkhouse produced a series of caricatures depicting academic life which were published in a Cambridge University magazine (c.1907). Agnes Conway, the secretary of the Women's Work Sub-committee of the Imperial War Museum, hadseen these drawings when she studied at the University. In 1917, she began making enquiries about Victoria Monkhouse. Conway wrote to a mutual acquaintance that she was looking around for 'a clever woman to do watercolour drawings of women war workers in all their different uniforms'. Monkhouse was subsequently commissioned by the Women's Work Sub-committee in 1919 to produce a series of drawings of women who had taken over the jobs of men to release them for front line duty, for which she charged £3 each.

Monkhouse later offered to produce war art during the Second World War, but this offer was not taken up.

Olive Mudie-Cooke (1890–1925)

Olive Mudie-Cooke studied art at St John's Wood Art School and then at Goldsmiths College, also spending time working in Venice. In January 1916 she and her sister Phyllis went to France with the First Aid Nursing Yeomanry (FANY). Mudie-Cooke drove ambulances for FANY and later for the Red Cross.

Mudie-Cooke was commissioned in 1919 by the Imperial War Museum's Women's Work Sub-committee to produce drawings depicting the work of the British Red Cross Voluntary Aid Detachment units in France.

After the war, she travelled widely, and in 1923 visited South Africa, where she exhibited some of her work. Mudie-Cooke returned briefly to England, but in 1925 returned to France, where she took her own life.

Stella Schmolle (1908–1975)

Born in Barnes, London, Stella Schmolle graduated from the Central School of Arts and Crafts in 1939. Before joining the Auxiliary Territorial Service (ATS) in 1942, she worked as an illustrator and commercial artist, exhibiting at the Royal Academy (RA) between 1938 and 1940.

In December 1941 Schmolle applied to work in the Ministry of Information's Art Department. She was not given a position, but it was recommended that she was given assistance by the War Artists Advisory Committee (WAAC) in obtaining facilities and materials to work as an artist, while engaged as a draughtswoman to an intelligence officer in the ATS. Schmolle was not officially commissioned by the WAAC, but the committee purchased seventeen of her pictures, including depictions of numerous ATS scenes in Britain, France and Belgium and – more unusually – a drawing of French collaborators at Vaucelles, Normandy.

After the war she taught art and became well known for her portraits. Her most notable work is her *Stations of the Cross*, commissioned for the Roman Catholic Chapel at the Royal Military Academy at Sandhurst. Her work is held in several collections including the Imperial War Museum, British Museum and Auckland Art Gallery.

Priscilla Thornycroft (b.1917)

Born in Golders Green, London, Priscilla Thornycroft studied at the Slade School of Fine Art, graduating in 1937. She was an active member of the Artists International Association, a left-wing artists' organisation, which she joined as a student, and was also a member of the Hogarth group of communist party artists. During this period she produced several notable anti-fascist posters for Spanish Civil War campaigns.

Thornycroft worked as a freelance illustrator. She was not an officially commissioned war artist and did not possess a drawing permit, but chose to sketch and paint the scenes she witnessed around her Camden Town studio in the early 1940s: children playing amongst the ruins of bombed buildings; women gathering in the streets; the newly-homeless and those who took shelter in the Underground during air raids. Her dark, humorous paintings show a world in which only the women, children and the elderly remain.

Travelling with her two young daughters, Thornycroft moved to the Soviet-occupied zone of Berlin to join her German husband in 1948. She later moved to Dresden, where several of her oil paintings are held in the city's museum. The artist donated several drawings to the Imperial War Museum in 1993 and some additional sketches and three oil paintings in 2009.

Official Commissions from the First World War to the Present Day

First World War: Female Artists Employed or Commissioned by the Imperial War Museum (IWM)

Artist	Dates	Details of Involvement
Anna Airy	1882–1964	Commissioned by the IWM's Ministry of Munitions Sub-committee for four paintings June 1918; Commissioned by the British War Memorials Committee for a large canvas September 1918, picture rejected January 1919; Commissioned by the IWM's Women's Work Sub-committee for one painting March 1919; Worked for the Canadian scheme
Clare Atwood	1886–1962	Considered by the British War Memorials Committee without outcome; Commissioned by the IWM Women's Work Sub-committee in 1919
Geneste Beeton	b.1880–?	Commissioned by the IWM Women's Work Sub-committee in 1920
Isabel Codrington	1874–1943	Commissioned by the IWM Women's Work Sub-committee in 1919
Dorothy Coke	1897–1979	Initial sketches for a British War Memorials Committee commission were rejected c.July/August 1918; Two watercolours were later purchased for the IWM by Sir Muirhead Bone
Tony Cyriax (Mrs Almgren)	Active 1914–20	Drawings commissioned by Sir Muirhead Bone in 1919 and presented to the IWM
Nellie Isaac		Commissioned by the IWM Women's Work Sub-committee in 1919
Lucy Kemp-Welch	1869–1958	Commissioned by the IWM Women's Work Sub-committee 1919–20
Phyllis Keyes		Commissioned by the IWM Women's Work Sub-committee in 1919
Beatrice Lithiby	b.1889–?	Commissioned by the IWM Women's Work Sub-committee in 1919
Victoria Monkhouse	?1883–19??	Commissioned by the IWM Women's Work Sub-committee 1918, 1919
Nora Neilson-Gray	1882–1931	Commissioned by the IWM Women's Work Sub-committee 1919–20

Derived from Sue Malvern, *Modern Art, Britain and the Great War, Witnessing, Testimony and Remembrance*, New Haven and London 2004, pp.181–6.

First World War: Female Artists Involved with Commissions from the British War Memorial Committee or the Ministry of Information (MOI)

Artist	Dates	Details of Involvement
Anna Airy	1882–1964	Commissioned by the IWM's Ministry of Munitions Sub-committee for four paintings June 1918; Commissioned by the British War Memorials Committee for a large canvas September 1918. Picture rejected January 1919; Commissioned by the IWM's Women's Work Sub-committee for one painting March 1919; Worked for the Canadian scheme
Clare Atwood	1886–1962	Approached for a British War Memorials Committee commission for a large canvas without outcome; Commissioned by Women's Work Section of the IWM February 1919; Worked for the Canadian scheme
Dorothy Coke	1897–1979	Initial sketches for a British War Memorials Committee commission were rejected c.July/August 1918, two watercolours were later purchased for the IWM by Sir Muirhead Bone
Dame Laura Knight	1877–1970	Approached by MOI (no outcome) and by the IWM; Women's Work Sub-committee (no outcome); Worked for the Canadian scheme
Flora Lion	1876–1958	Contributed a portrait of Lavery to British Artists at the Front; Approached by the MOI and asked to produce some work based on visits to munitions factories. Finished work October 1918, but it was not purchased. Later the work was donated to the IWM; Worked for the Canadian scheme
Annie Swynnerton ARA	1844–1933	Approached by MOI. No outcome
Margaret Lindsay Williams	1888–1960	Approached MOI. Rejected

Derived from Sue Malvern, *Modern Art, Britain and the Great War, Witnessing, Testimony and Remembrance*, New Haven and London 2004, pp.181–6.

Second World War: Female Artists whose Work was Acquired by the War Artists Advisory Committee (WAAC)

Artist	Dates	Details of Acquisition
Enid Abrahams	1906–1972	Independent submission to the WAAC, one work acquired
Mary Adshead	1904–1995	Independent submission to the WAAC, one work acquired
Griselda Allan	1905–1987	Independent submission to the WAAC, one work acquired
Rosemary Allan	1911–2009	Short-term contract, four works acquired
Kathleen Saywell Allen	1906–1983	Independent submission to the WAAC, one work acquired
Doris Blair	Active 1940s–90s	Independent submission to the WAAC, two works acquired
Norma Bull	1906–1980	Independent submission to the WAAC, three works acquired
Daphne Chart	Active 1930–41	Independent submission to the WAAC, one work acquired
Malvina Cheek	b.1915–	Independent submission to the WAAC, one work acquired
Dora Clarke	1895–1989	Short-term contract, one work acquired
Dorothy Coke	1897–1979	Short-term contract, eight works acquired
Joy Collier	Unknown	Independent submission to the WAAC, two works acquired
Joan Connew	b.1915–?	Independent submission to the WAAC, one work acquired
Evelyn Dunbar	1906–1960	Full-time salaried artist; Commissioned by the WAAC for six Women's Voluntary Services subjects in March 1940. Four finally accepted; Commission to paint nursing subjects August 1941; Six-month salaried commission October 1942; Six-month salaried commission September 1943; Six-month salaried commission March 1944; In total forty works were acquired by the WAAC
Pamela Dunton	Unknown	Independent submission to the WAAC, one work acquired
Leila Faithfull	1898–1994	Independent submission to the WAAC, three works acquired
Victorine Foot	1920–2000	Independent submission to the WAAC, one work acquired
Mollie Forestier-Walker	1912–c.1990	Independent submission to the WAAC, one work acquired
Ethel Gabain	1882–1950	Short-term contract. Thirty-eight works acquired by the WAAC, some of these were lithographs and were acquired in multiple
Kaff [Katherine] Gerrard	1894–1970	Independent submission to the WAAC, one work acquired
Evelyn Gibbs	1905–1991	Short-term contract, seven works acquired by the WAAC
Phyllis Ginger	1907–2005	Independent submission to the WAAC. One work acquired. This work was given to the Worshipful Company of Goldsmiths, who then commissioned a second picture for the WAAC
Grace Golden	1904–1993	Independent submission to the WAAC, one work acquired
Kathleen Guthrie	1905–1981	Independent submission to the WAAC, one work acquired
Hilda Harrisson	1888–1972	Independent submission to the WAAC, two works acquired
Rose Henriques	1877–1972	Independent submission to the WAAC, one work acquired
Elsie Hewland	1901–1979	Independent submission to the WAAC, five works acquired
Ray Howard-Jones	1903–1996	Short-term contract, fifteen works acquired by the WAAC
Eleanor (Erlund) Hudson	b.1912	Independent submission to the WAAC, six works acquired
Ruth Hurle	Active 1930s–40s	Independent submission to the WAAC, one work acquired
Mabel Hutchinson	Active 1930s–40s	Independent submission to the WAAC, one work acquired
Barbara Jones	1912–1978	Independent submission to the WAAC, one work acquired
Pegaret Keeling	1915–2000	Independent submission to the WAAC, one work acquired
Mary Kessell	1914–1977	Short-term contract, twenty-six works acquired by the WAAC
Eve Kirk	1900–1969	Independent submission to the WAAC, two works acquired
Dame Laura Knight	1877–1970	Short-term contract, seventeen works acquired by the WAAC
Nora Lavrin	1897–1985	Independent submission to the WAAC, four works acquired
Olga Lehmann	1912–2001	Independent submission to the WAAC, two works acquired
Frances Macdonald	1914–2002	Short-term contract, nineteen works acquired by the WAAC
Violet Baber Mimpriss	1895–1987	Independent submission to the WAAC, three works acquired
		Continues overleaf

Mona Moore	1917–2000	Short-term contract, six works acquired by the WAAC
Elizabeth Polunin	1877–1950	Short-term contract, one work acquired by the WAAC
Patricia Preece	1894–1966	Short-term contract, one work acquired by the WAAC
Louisa Puller	b.1885–?	Independent submission to the WAAC, two works acquired
Stella Schmolle	1908–1975	Independent submission to the WAAC, seventeen works acquired
Felicity Sutton	Unknown	Independent submission to the WAAC, one work acquired
Paule Vézelay	1892–1984	Independent submission to the WAAC, one work acquired
Barbara Watson	Active 1940s	Independent submission to the WAAC, one work acquired
Kaete [Katerina] Wilczynski	1894–1978	Independent submission to the WAAC, one work acquired
Anne F Wilson	b.1927–?	Independent submission to the WAAC, one work acquired
Anna Zinkeisen	1901–1976	Independent submission to the WAAC, one work acquired
Doris Zinkeisen	1898–1991	Offered a short-term contract but chose to submit work independently. Five works acquired. Four of these were produced while Zinkesien was an artist for the Red Cross

Derived from Brian Foss, *War Paint: Art, War, State and Identity in Britain, 1939–1945*, London 2007, pp.196–204.
Additional details researched and compiled by Sara Bevan.

Female Artists Commissioned by the Artistic Records Committee or Artistic Commissions Committee of the Imperial War Museum (IWM)

Artist	Dates	Subject Matter	Title	Date of Commission
Helen Lee	b.1951	Duxford Airfield	*Duxford Airfield; Aeroplane at Duxford, 1978*	1978
Lady Kinahan	Unknown	UDR Northern Ireland	*9th UDR Signal Exercise, Overlooking Belfast Dock*	1980
Linda Kitson	b.1945	Falklands Conflict	60 drawings acquired	1982
Eileen Hogan	b.1946	Women's Services: WRNS [Women's Royal Naval Service]	*WRN Air Mechanic, Portland 1983; WRN Air Mechanic Jan Lions, Portland 1983; Tennis: The Royal Naval Hospital, Haslar; WRN Air Mechanic, Portland 1983; Coronary Care Ward, Royal Naval Hospital, Haslar 1983*	1983
Boyd and Evans (Fionnula Boyd and Leslie Evans)	b.1944 [Boyd]; b.1945 [Evans]	Women's Services: WRAF [Women's Royal Air Force]	*Bird Scarer R.A.F. Lyneham 1984–5; Airload Master Checking Engines, R.A.F. Lyneham 1985; Security Check on the Pan, R.A.F. Lyneham 1985; Airload Master Carrying out Pre-Flight Check on the Airfield, R.A.F. Lyneham 1985; In-Flight Check, Hercules, R.A.F. Lyneham; Checking Between Flights, Wessex Helicopter, R.A.F. Shawbury 1985*	1984
Sonia Lawson	b.1934	BAOR [British Army of the Rhine]	*Two Minds But with a Single Thought?; Troops in Single File Prepare to Break Cover and Board a Chinook Helicopter; Camouflaged Men in a Trench; Men Disguised as Clods*	1984
Maggi Hambling	b.1945	Women's Services: WRAC [Women's Royal Army Corps]	*The Staff Band of the Women's Royal Army Corps, 1984; Captain E.P. Forster WRAC, Director of Music, WRAC Staff Band, 1984*	1984
Jane Stanton	b.1958	Women's Services: WRAC [Women's Royal Army Corps]	*Wounded from Crete; Double Fracture 1943; An Emergency Operation in a Hospital Ward, Athens, 1941; A Cattle-truck Journey from Salonika to Germany, 1941*	1985
Deanna Petherbridge	b.1939	Aircraft Production	*Debris of War 1984; Boeing Assembly Plant, Seattle 1989*	1989
Langlands & Bell (Ben Langlands and Nikki Bell)	b.1955 [Langlands]; b.1959 [Bell]	The aftermath of the September 11 attacks and the War in Afghanistan	*Zardad's Dog, NGOs* [both from the project: *The House of Osama Bin Laden*]	2002
Susan Philipsz	b.1965	Imperial War Museum Duxford	*From a Distance* [site-specific project]	2007

Further Reading

Archival Sources

Artists' papers and oral history interviews, Documents and Sound Section, Imperial War Museum.

Magdalen Evans, 'Biography of Erlund Hudson', n.d., artist file, Art Section, Imperial War Museum.

Magdalen Evans, Obituary: Phyllis Ginger, the *Independent*, 10 May 2005.

The War Artists Archive, Art Section, Imperial War Museum.

Women's Work Collection, Library, Imperial War Museum.

Art and War

Fionna Barber and Megan Johnston, *Archiving Place and Time: Contemporary Art Practice in Northern Ireland Since the Belfast Agreement*, Portadown 2009.

Laura Brandon, *Art or Memorial?: The Forgotten History of Canada's War Art*, Calgary 2006.

Laura Brandon, *Art and War*, London 2009.

Toby Clark, *Art and Propaganda in the Twentieth Century*, revised edn., London and New York 1997.

David Peters Corbett, *The Modernity of English Art, 1914–30*, Manchester 1997.

Richard Cork, *A Bitter Truth: Avant-Garde Art and the Great War*, New Haven and London 1994.

Brian Foss, *War Paint: Art, War, State and Identity in Britain, 1939–1945*, New Haven and London 2007.

Meirion Harries and Susie Harries, *The War Artists: British Official War Art of the Twentieth Century*, London 1983.

Sue Malvern, *Modern Art, Britain and the Great War, Witnessing, Testimony and Remembrance*, New Haven and London 2004.

Ulrike Smalley, 'Objective Realists – British War Artists as Witnesses to the Liberation of Bergen-Belsen Concentration Camp', *The Holocaust in History and Memory*, vol. 2, 2009, pp.53–67.

Catherine Speck, *Painting Ghosts: Australian Women Artists in Wartime*, London and Sydney 2003.

Val Williams, *Warworks: Women, Photography and the Iconography of War*, London 1994.

Individual Artists

Anna Airy: Retrospective Loan Exhibition, Oils, Water-Colours, Pastels, Etchings, Drawings, Ipswich 1985.

Ronald Alley (ed.), *Paule Vézelay*, London 1983.

Fiona Banner, Gregory Burke and Cay-Sophie Rabinowitz, *The Bastard Word*, Toronto 2007.

Cheryl Brutvan, 'Sophie Ristelhueber's Obsessions', *Sophie Ristelhueber: Details of the World*, Boston 2001.

Jane Carmichael, 'Olive Edis: Imperial War Museum Photographer in France and Belgium, March 1919', *Imperial War Museum Review*, no.4, 1984, pp.4–11.

Gill Clarke, *Evelyn Dunbar – War and Country*, Bristol 2006.

Robert Campbell, 'An Emotive Place Apart', *American Institute of Architects Journal*, May 1983, p.151.

Mladen Dolar, Anselem Franke et al., *Smadar Dreyfus*, Stockholm 2009.

Janet Dunbar, *Laura Knight*, London 1975.

Jane England, *Paule Vézelay 1892 – 1984: Retrospective Exhibition*, London 2004.

P. Kelleway, *Highly Desirable: The Zinkeisen Sisters and Their Legacy*, Suffolk 2008.

Linda Kitson, *The Falklands War: A Visual Diary*, London 1982.

Laura Knight, *Oil Paint and Grease Paint: the Autobiography of Laura Knight*, London 1936.

Ben Langlands and Nikki Bell, *The House of Osama Bin Laden*, London 2004.

Pauline Lucas, *Evelyn Gibbs: Artist and Traveller*, Nottingham 2001.

Susan Thompson, *The Life and Works of Ethel Gabain*, Manchester 2008.

Laura Wortley, *Lucy Kemp-Welch 1869–1958: The Spirit of the Horse*, London 1996.

Women as Artists

Carol Armstrong and Catherine de Zegher, *Women Artists at the Millennium*, London and Cambridge, Massachussets 2006.

Frances Borzello, *A World of Our Own – Women as Artists*, London 2000.

Karen Brown (ed.), *Women's Contributions to Visual Culture*, 1918–1939, Aldershot 2008.

Whitney Chadwick, *Women, Art and Society*, 4th edn., London 2007.

Katy Deepwell, *Dialogues: Women Artists from Ireland*, London 2005.

Katy Deepwell, *Women Artists Between The Wars – 'A fair field and no favour'*, Manchester 2010.

Rebecca Fortnum, *Contemporary British Women Artists*, London 2007.

Alicia Foster, *Tate Women Artists*, London 2004.

Germaine Greer, *The Obstacle Race: The Fortunes of Women Painters and Their Work*, 2nd edn., London 2001.

Camille Morineau et al., *Women Artists – elles@centrepompidou*, Paris 2009.

Linda Nochlin, *Women, Art and Power and Other Essays*, Boulder, Colorado 1988.

Roszika Parker and Griselda Pollock, *Old Mistresses; Women, Art and Ideology*, London 1981.

Griselda Pollock, *Vision and Difference: Femininity, Feminism, and Histories of Art*, London and New York 1987.

Women, War and Culture

Kate Adie, *Corsets to Camouflage: Women and War*, London 2003.

Joanna Bourke, *Dismembering the Male: Men's Bodies, Britain and the Great War*, London 1996.

Gail Braybon and Penny Summerfield, *Out of the Cage: Women's Experiences in Two World Wars*, London 1987.

Gail Braybon, *Women Workers in the First World War*, London 1981.

Vera Brittain, *Testament of Youth: An Autobiographical Study of the Years 1900–1925*, London 1933.

Angus Calder, *The People's War*, London 1969.

Diana M. Condell, 'The Imperial War Museum 1917–1920: a Study of the Institution and its Presentation of the First World War', M Phil thesis, Council for National Academic Awards 1985.

Diana M. Condell and Jean Liddiard, *Working for Victory? Images of Women in the First World War, 1914–18*, London 1987.

Mark Connelly, *We Can Take It! Britain and the Memory of the Second World War*, London 2004.

Mark Donnelly, *Britain in the Second World War*, London 1999.

Nigel Fountain and Laurie Milner (ed.), *Women at War*, London 2002.

Susan R. Grayzel, *Women and the First World War*, Harlow 2002.

Susan R. Grayzel, *Women's Identities at War: Gender, Motherhood, and Politics in Britain and France During the First World War*, Chapel Hill, North Carolina 1999.

Susan R Grayzel (ed.), *Women, Work and Society 1914–1918*, Cengage resource based on the Women's Work Collection at the Imperial War Museum. <http://www.tlemea.com/introduction.asp> (accessed 12 Nov. 2010).

Samuel Hynes, *A War Imagined: The First World War and English Culture*, London 1990.

Arthur Marwick, *Women at War 1914–1918*, London 1977.

Lucy Noakes, *Women in the British Army: War and the Gentle Sex, 1907–48*, London 2006.

Gill Plain, *Women's Fiction of the Second World War: Gender, Power and Resistance*, Edinburgh 1996.

Catherine W. Reilly (ed.), *Chaos of the Night: Women's Poetry and Verse of the Second World War*, London 1984.

Angela K. Smith (ed.), *Women's Writing of the First World War: an Anthology*, Manchester 2000.

Penny Summerfield, *Women Workers in the Second World War: Production and Patriarchy in Conflict*, London 1984.

Deborah Thom, *Nice Girls and Rude Girls: Women Workers in World War One*, London 2000.

Dan Todman, *The Great War: Myth and Memory*, London 2005.

Mary Wilkinson, 'Patriotism and Duty: the Women's Work Collection at the Imperial War Museum', *The Imperial War Museum Review*, no. 6, 1991, pp.31–37.

Angela Woollacott, *On Her Their Lives Depend: Munitions Workers in the First World War*, Berkeley, California 1994.

Quotations:

Diary of Mary Kessell reproduced by kind permission of the artist's family.

Extract from 'Afghan Diary' from *The House of Osama Bin Laden* courtesy the artists.

Scarred Landscapes: interview with Sophie Ristelhueber (*Art World*, issue 11, June/July 2009). Available online at <http://www.foto8.com/new/online/blog/967sophie ristelhueber interviewed>

Mona Hatoum in conversation with Janine Antoni. This interview was commissioned by and first published in *BOMB Magazine*, *BOMB* #63, Spring 1998, pp. 61–64. © *Bomb Magazine*, New Art Publications, and its Contributors. All rights reserved. The BOMB Digital Archive can be viewed at www.bombsite.com. With thanks to *BOMB Magazine* and the artist.

Extract from Doris Zinkeisen's autobiography reproduced by kind permission of the artist's son.

Extract from Paule Vézelay's correspondence reproduced by kind permission of the artist's niece and England & Co. gallery.

Text from Frauke Eigen's portfolio reproduced by kind permission of the artist.

Image List

vi.   IWM ART 17438. Watercolour and conté crayon. 630 x 475mm. Reproduced by kind permission of the artist

6.   IWM ART 3051. Watercolour on brown paper. 292 x 215mm

8.   IWM ART 5398. Watercolour. 311 x 238mm

9.   IWM ART 5401. Watercolour. 241 x 330mm

10.   IWM Q 8063

11.   IWM Q 8117

12.   N03217 © Tate, 2011. Oil on canvas. 1524 x 3061mm. By kind permission of David Messum

14.   IWM ART LD 5745 d. Sanguine. 203 x 254mm

15.   (t) IWM ART LD 5750. Charcoal. 488 x 618mm
(bl) IWM ART LD 5752 b. Charcoal. 342 x 320mm

16.   IWM ART LD 5798. Oil on canvas. 1828 x 1524mm

17.   IWM ART LD 4993. Watercolour. 304 x 460mm

18.   IWM ART 15530 52. Conté crayon. 355 x 253mm

20.   (t) IWM ART 15530 50. Conté crayon and coloured oil pastel. 296 x 421mm
(bl) IWM ART 15530 63. Ink (red marker pen) on paper. 502 x 327mm

22.   *Zardad's Dog* [film still] © Langlands & Bell. Courtesy the artists

23.   *Beirut, photographs*, Sophie Ristelhueber, 1984. Black and white photograph, silver print. 50 x 60. © Sophie Ristelhueber / adagp Paris

24.   (t) *Iraq 2001* [Part of a triptych] Sophie Ristelhueber, 2001. Colour photograph, chromogenic print mounted on aluminium. 120 x 180. © Sophie Ristelhueber / adagp Paris
(bl) IWM ART 1146. Oil on canvas. 711 x 914mm

25.   *Veil 1*, Mary McIntyre. Colour Lightjet Photographic print. 100 x 80cm. Courtesy the artist and the Third Space Gallery

26.   IWM ART LD 3349. Oil on canvas. 609 x 457mm

28.   IWM ART 2314. Pencil and watercolour on paper. 477 x 338mm

29.   (t) IWM ART 3160. Oil on canvas. 1828 x 3962mm. By kind permission of David Messum
(b) IWM ART 2852. Oil on canvas. 1847 x 2171mm

30.   IWM ART LD 1443. Oil on canvas. 762 x 635mm

32.   (t) IWM ART LD 3523. Watercolour. 310 x 461mm. (bl) IWM ART LD 2596. Watercolour on paper. 230 x 264mm. (br) IWM ART LD 1430. Ink wash. 368 x 530mm

33.   IWM ART LD 626. Oil on canvas. 914 x 609mm

34.   IWM ART 3062. Oil on canvas. 1524 x 1828mm

36.   (t) N05688 © Tate, 2011. Oil on canvas. 914 x 1829mm
(b) IWM ART LD 3987. Oil on canvas. 622 x 1828mm

37.   IWM ART 17421. Watercolour and ink. 310 x 450mm

38.   IWM ART LD 2992. Watercolour. 584 x 466mm. Reproduced by kind permission of the artist

39.   (l) IWM ART 17438. Watercolour and conté crayon. 630 x 475mm. Reproduced by kind permission of the artist
(r) *For Alice Hunter* © Rozanne Hawksley. Mixed media, primarily cloth, thread, metal. By kind permission of the artist. Photographs: Philip Clarke

40.   (t) IWM ART 3090. Oil on canvas. 1143 x 1397mm
(bl) IWM ART LD 3588. Pencil and wash. 552 x 742mm
(br) IWM ART LD 4217. Oil on canvas 622 x 749mm

42.   (t) IWM ART LD 3850. Oil on canvas. 622 x 749mm
(bl) IWM ART LD 6001. Oil on canvas. 711 x 914mm

43.   IWM ART LD 2478. Oil on canvas. 914 x 1524mm

44.   IWM ART LD 3016. Oil on canvas. 508 x 609mm

45.   (bl) IWM ART 16515 13. Ink and wash. 275 x 201mm
(br) IWM ART 16515 1. Pencil on tracing paper. 323 x 396mm

46.   (t) IWM ART 4435. Oil on canvas. 1076 x 1842mm
(b) IWM ART 4032. Oil on canvas. 1828 x 2133mm

48.   (t) IWM ART LD 2850. Oil on canvas. 863 x 1019mm
(b) IWM ART 17038. Ink and wash. 177 x 431mm. By kind permission of the artist's family

49.   IWM ART 17050. Watercolour pencil on paper. 280 x 190mm

50.   N05705 © Tate, 2011. Oil on canvas. 561 x 1220 x 17mm

51.   M00467_H © Tate, 2011. Installation. Courtesy the artist and Frith Street Gallery, London

52.   (t) *Dessert* © Rita Duffy. By kind permission of the artist. Photographer Cris Hill
(b) *Nature morte aux grenades*, Mona Hatoum, 2006–2007. Crystal, steel and rubber, 37 3/8 x 81 7/8 x 27 9/16 in. (95 x 208 x 70 cm). © the artist. Photo: Marc Domage. Courtesy Galerie Chantal Crousel, Paris

54.   *The Gray Drape*, 2008, Martha Rosler. Courtesy the artist and Galerie Christian Nagel

56.   (t) IWM ART LD 5468. Oil on canvas. 804 x 1000mm
(b) IWM ART LD 5584. Watercolour. 330 x 609mm

57.   N05718_H © Tate, 2011. Oil and pencil on canvas laid on wood. 762 x 635mm

58.   (t) IWM ART 16528 1. Lithograph. 278 x 347mm
(b) IWM ART 17474. Oil on board. 357 x 465mm

59.   IWM ART 17310. Lithograph. 320 x 450mm

61.   IWM ART LD 7206. Pencil and chalk. 647 x 501mm

62.   (t) IWM ART LD 264. Lithograph. 454 x 511mm
(bl) IWM ART 15221 7. Pencil. 278 x 225mm
(bm) IWM ART 15221 28. Pencil. 272 x 224mm
(br) IWM ART 15221 41. Pencil. 297 x 228mm

63.   *Every One 14*, Sophie Ristelhueber, 1994. Black and white photograph, silver print. 290 x 180. Unique, collection Victoria & Albert Museum, London. © Sophie Ristelhueber / adagp Paris

64.   (tl) IWM ART 16804 8, (tr) IWM ART 16804 3, (ml) IWM ART 16804 1, (mr) IWM ART 16804 12. All four Silver Gelatin Print. 500 x 500mm. Reproduced by kind permission of the artist
(b) *Measures of Distance*, Mona Hatoum, 1988. Colour video, sound, 15 minutes. © the artist. A western Front Video Production, Vancouver. Courtesy White Cube

66.   IWM ART 16737 © Jannane Al-Ani. Five channel video installation. Fifteen minutes. By kind permission of the artist and Rose Issa Projects

67.   *Veil* (Interior Detail), Rita Duffy. S125. Mixed media, prison doors, salt and glass. 6 doors, 185 x 169cm. Collection: Wolverhampton Arts & Heritage (Wolverhampton Art Gallery). Purchased with assistance from the National Art Collections Fund and the V&A Purchase Grant Fund, 2005. Copyright the artist. Supported by Armagh District Council. With thanks to the artist and Wolverhampton Art Gallery

68.   *Allegiances and Assurances*, Sandra Johnston. Three part video installation, variable size. Courtesy the artist and Third Space Gallery

69.   *Mother's Day, 2006–2008*, Smadar Dreyfus. Three channel HD video with 5.1 channel audio. Audiovisual installation, 15 minutes, 8 x 25m. Stills from video courtesy the artist

70.   (t) *Tron (Amputee)* from the series *House Beautiful: Bringing the War Home (1967–1972)*, Martha Rosler. Courtesy the artist and Galerie Christian Nagel
(b) *The Nature of the Beast*, Goshka Macuga, 2009. Installation view, The Bloomberg Commission, Whitechapel Gallery. Courtesy of the Whitechapel Gallery and Kate MacGarry, London. Photo: Patrick Lears

73.   (t) *The Thinking Soldier*, Kathleen Scott. Photo courtesy of Jennifer Sarabia
(bl) Vietnam Veterans' Memorial, Competition Drawing, Maya Lin, c.1980. Library of Congress, Prints & Photographs Division, Vietnam Veterans' Memorial Fund Slide Collection, LC-DIG-ppmsca-09504
(br) Vietnam Veterans' Memorial at Washington DC. Image no: CB058229. © L. Clarke/Corbis

74.   Holocaust Memorial, Judenplatz, Vienna, Rachel Whiteread, 2000. Concrete, 390 x 752 x 1058cm. Courtesy of the artist, Luhring Augustine, New York and Gagosian Gallery

75.   IWM ART 16410. Plastic and textile funeral flowers, silk, bone, silk padding, metal frame. 51mm, diameter. Reproduced by kind permission of the artist

76.   IWM ART 2316. Pencil and watercolour on paper. 393 x 279mm

Index